D0251331

blue
rider
press

WALK THIS WAY

Run-DMC, Aerosmith, and the Song That Changed American Music Forever

GEOFF EDGERS

Blue Rider Press
New York

blue
rider
press

An imprint of Penguin Random House LLC
penguinrandomhouse.com

LIBRARY OF CONGRESS CATALOGING-IN-PUBLICATION DATA
Names: Edgers, Geoff, author.
Title: Walk this way : Run-DMC, Aerosmith, and the song that changed American music forever / Geoff Edgers.
Description: New York : Blue Rider Press, [2019]
Identifiers: LCCN 2018045167| ISBN 9780735212237 (hardcover) | ISBN 9780735212251 (ebook)
Subjects: LCSH: Run-D.M.C. (Musical group) | Aerosmith (Musical group) | Rap musicians—United States—Biography. | Rock musicians—United States—Biography. | Run-D.M.C. (Musical group). Walk this way. | Aerosmith (Musical group). Walk this way (Song)
Classification: LCC ML421.R84 W35 2019 | DDC 782.42166092/2 [B] —dc23 LC record available at https://lccn.loc.gov/2018045167

Printed in the United States of America

10 9 8 7 6 5 4 3 2 1

Book design by Francesca Belanger

Insert photo credits appear on page 271.
Interior images: pages iv–v: Danny Sanchez;
page 13: courtesy of Sal Abbatiello;
page 151: photo by Lloyd Nelson, courtesy of Bill Adler.

To Carlene, Lila and Calvin. You put up with so much.
I hope I can someday pay a little of it back.

CONTENTS

CAST OF CHARACTERS

Run-DMC

Joseph Simmons (Run)—Run-DMC's most vocal member and considered the MC who formed the group. Also the younger brother of manager and hip-hop mogul Russell Simmons.

Darryl McDaniels (DMC)—The comic book geek whose deep voice and imaginative rhymes earn him a spot as Run's partner on the mic.

Jason Mizell (Jam Master Jay)—Added after Run-DMC's first album, Mizell is a serviceable DJ who becomes a master on the turntable and, more importantly, serves as a powerful influence when Run and DMC aren't taking the task at hand seriously.

Rick Rubin, producer—The NYU student who starts the record label Def Jam Recordings in his dorm room and earns respect for his stripped-down productions at a time when so many rappers are being forced to use disco-style instrumentation.

Russell Simmons, producer, manager—The second of three Simmons brothers, he starts his career as a concert promoter before launching Rush Management and representing rap pioneer Kurtis Blow. Will eventually join Rubin to partner on Def Jam Recordings.

Larry Smith, producer—A bassist by training, Smith would produce Kurtis Blow, the Fat Boys, Whodini, and Run-DMC. His tragic decline and early death left him all but forgotten. But over a five-year period, he produced some of rap's most successful albums.

Bill Adler, journalist, band publicist/biographer—Adler was among the first journalists to write appreciatively about hip-hop. In 1984, he signed on to become director of publicity for Russell Simmons and Def Jam, spearheading campaigns for Run-DMC, LL Cool J, Whodini, and Public Enemy during the next half-dozen years.

Cory Robbins and Steve Plotnicki, cofounders, Profile Records—They were not the first to put out rap records, but Robbins and Plotnicki were the first to see the potential of rap albums. And unlike many indie companies, they were reluctant to let go of their acts once they became popular.

Aerosmith

Steven Tyler—Aerosmith's lead singer, spark plug, and resident diva. He was Jagger to Joe Perry's Richards, a flamboyant front man who could also play piano and drums. He and Perry would be known as the Toxic Twins because of their drug use.

Joe Perry—Aerosmith's lead guitarist. Quiet, mysterious, and hard to get close to. He would be responsible for writing many of the group's signature riffs, including the central hook of "Walk This Way."

Jimmy Crespo and Rick Dufay—When Perry and Brad Whitford exit, Aerosmith brings in a new pair of guitarists. Crespo is a masterful player eager to revive the group, but shy and fragile. Dufay is a madman, brash and argumentative and not afraid to talk back or even tackle Tyler.

Tim Collins—A small-time manager who meets Joe Perry when the guitarist is at his lowest point and gets him back on the road and a record deal. When Perry approaches the other Aerosmith members to reform, he does it on one condition: Collins has to be their manager.

John Kalodner—The superstar A&R man, known for his Lennonesque appearance (white suits, long hair, and flowing beard), signs Aerosmith to Geffen Records after they reform and then finds himself under fire when he can't control the rebellious band.

Jack Douglas—The producer who transformed Aerosmith from a local band to stadium kings. Responsible for the band's greatest works, including "Walk This Way" and "Sweet Emotion" and brought back to try to salvage the Perryless *Rock in a Hard Place*.

WALK THIS WAY

INTRODUCTION

Run-DMC made it possible for all the majors to see that rap music and hip-hop was album-oriented music and rap artists were rock stars, really. Run-DMC was the complete sacrifice for anything that was successful after 1986.

—Chuck D

The collaborators were, until that March morning in 1986, total strangers. You'll hear Tyler try to tell you otherwise, boasting about those mixtapes he would pick up when he was living in New York City in the early '80s. And that may be true. But even if he was digging all those B-boy jams, Tyler's true focus had nothing to do with music. He was a dope fiend on a twenty-dollar-a-day allowance. He certainly wasn't checking out the Cold Crush.

And his partner, Joe Perry? The guitarist at least had a kid in the house to introduce him to this new sound. His stepson, Aaron, just thirteen years old, had tapes from the Fat Boys, Doug E. Fresh, Grandmaster Flash and the Furious Five, and, of course, Run-DMC. Did Perry fall in love with hip-hop? Not exactly. But the kid's stack of tapes at least introduced him to the whirlpool of sonic energy.

To Tyler and Perry's credit, at least they pretended to know the guys. That was just good manners. Joey "Run" Simmons and Darryl "DMC" McDaniels, seventeen years younger than both Aerosmith leaders, didn't seem particularly concerned about showing mutual respect. They were smart-ass kids, late for the session and reluctant to be there in the first place. It was left to Jason Mizell, better known as Jam Master Jay, to tell Run and D that they better hustle down to the studio and take a serious whack at the song. Even then, they huddled on the couch with Big Macs, grumbling something about a stolen car. They hadn't even memorized the words to the song they were being asked to do, a song that had been a staple of 1970s white-programmed FM radio. They just knew the beat. "Give us number four on *Toys in the Attic*," they'd say, no clue that there was a band—one of the biggest in the country—behind it.

Those were the two sides: a pair of pale-faced rockers itching for a fix, a trio of black kids still trying to figure out why they were there. What none of them understood is that together, in a single Sunday afternoon in Manhattan, they would change not just music but society itself.

That's not just hyperbole. Before Run-DMC covered "Walk This Way," there was no *Yo! MTV Raps*, no *Arsenio*, no *In Living Color.* What's more, hip-hop was not part of the twenty-four-hour video network's rotation, and it was never, ever played on mainstream radio.

It had all begun in February 1986 when Run-DMC thought they were basically done with their third album. Then, Rick Rubin, the producer, decided he needed something else. He wanted to turn Run-DMC into more than the most popular rap group in the world. He wanted the big tent, the wider reach, suburbia. The next step seemed natural. Take a staple of rock (i.e., white) radio—Aerosmith's 1975 hit "Walk This Way"—and turn it into hip-hop. This wasn't just a random dart thrown at Casey Kasem's board. Rubin genuinely loved Aerosmith. He had also already employed the rock-rap blueprint on another production, the debut rap single for the then unknown Beastie Boys. "Rock Hard," released in 1984, featured a sample of the crunching, central riff from AC/DC's "Back in Black."

The idea of doing a cover song didn't make a bit of sense to Run or to DMC. They didn't do covers. Nobody did.

Rubin had started with a homework assignment: Learn the real words to "Walk This Way." This was 1986, long before Google searches or Genius annotations, so lyric-gathering would need to be done the hard way. Rubin pulled out Aerosmith's 1975 album, *Toys in the Attic*, gave the guys a yellow notepad, and told them to put on song four. Listen. Write.

The words?

Backstroke lover always hidin' 'neath the cover,
Still I talked to your daddy he say.

Whaaa?!

Run and D didn't know the song had gone Top 10 or had been a radio staple. They knew the song for just the first four seconds, the hottest of breakbeats. Any DJ worth his Technics 1200 would cut it before the guitar arrived. The guys had heard that beat in park jams and on some of the homemade tapes sold on the street. They didn't even know the name of the song, only where it fell on the record. Standing there, in front of the DJ, an MC's shorthand wouldn't even mention "Walk This Way" as they launched into the next routine.

"We were going for the beats," said Run. "We would say,

'Pick up that joint from *Toys in the Attic* and scratch the beginning.' If you got past that, the DJ made a huge mistake."

Bom BAT, be boom-boom BAT.

White suburban kids in garage bands were banging out Black Sabbath's "Paranoid" or Led Zeppelin's "Whole Lotta Love" on their knockoff Strats. Club DJs had their own staples. They dropped the needle on Billy Squier's "The Big Beat," Bob James's "Take Me to the Mardi Gras," or the opening to "Walk."

Today, you can hear the evidence. On YouTube, it's easy to track down Grandmaster Flash sampling the Aerosmith "Walk" as early as 1978—eight years before Rubin hands Run and D the yellow notepad. The sound clip illustrates exactly how he became Flash. So fast, he wouldn't let that beat get too far.

Except, on that day, in a basement across the city, Run and D were following orders, and those orders required them to let the groove slide past the break, through the funky guitar, and damn, can you believe this wack shit? Some spazzy white dude double-talking through verses that might as well have been the Norwegian national anthem.

Singin' hey diddle-diddle with the kitty in the middle

That voice was Steven Tyler's. Seventies rock hero, groupie-guzzler, doper, motormouth, wearer of sausage-snuggling tights. Joe Perry played guitar. Close your eyes and you can sniff the smoke wafting from the cigarette suspended in his headstock as his fingers fly across the fretboard of his Les Paul. These guys were not brothers; they were the Toxic Twins, drinking, smoking, snorting, chomping, shooting anything that entered their Venn diagram of self-destruction. For a while, these appetites seemed to serve them well, or at least to not get in their way. They were the American Stones, selling millions of records and packing seventy-thousand-seat stadiums with members of their Blue Army—working-class kids in jeans and matching denim jackets swaying to "Sweet Emotion," "Dream On," and "Walk This Way."

But this was 1986. By this point, they were barely hanging on. These weren't rock stars. They were confused, damaged souls coming off a failed comeback record that was threatening to land them in classic rock jail.

Rick Rubin didn't think about that stuff. His drug of choice was the General Tso's chicken that flowed into his dorm room, and he remained in awe of Tyler and Perry. Yes, the producer was running a record label out of room 712 of New York University's Weinstein Hall. When a buddy from NYU suggested that Aerosmith's fortunes had dropped so low that they would consider a collaboration with a rap group, Rubin was stunned. "You really think they'll do it?" he said.

For $8,000, they would. Now if only Run and D would cooperate.

At least Jay got it. The DJ was in the middle, at the studio, still trying to get them to pick up the phone. As the guy on the turntables, he was used to being in the background as Run and D pranced around the stage. On their last record, Jay wasn't even on the cover. That's a crime. At twenty-one, Jay was a few months younger than Joey and Darryl but came off as the older soul. He was the connector, communicator, and taskmaster. He was also the peacemaker, a role not properly recognized until he was gone and peace was so hard to come by. Jay could already imagine a life outside Run-DMC. That's why he was a studio rat, watching Rubin and the engineers, knowing that one day, he, too, wanted to run the board.

"Hell no, this ain't going to happen," Run insisted when he finally picked up the phone.

Tyler's lyrics didn't exactly speak to him.

"This is hillbilly gibberish," Run complained. "Country bumpkin bullshit."

He could hear his older brother in the background.

"Motherfucking Joey!" Russell yelled.

Run had heard enough. He handed the phone to D, now the target of their manager's frustration.

"Darryl, you stupid motherfucker for following him!" Russell yelled.

They stayed away. For how long? In some stories, it's a week, which doesn't really make any sense. Sometimes, it's just hours. Nobody really remembered. There were no cell phones, no stamped texts, nothing but memories made foggy by age, malt liquor, and weed. What we do know is that eventually a call led to a détente.

"Jay, where you at?" DMC asked, now calm.

There was something they should know, Jay told them. Rubin had somehow convinced the guys on the record to come into the studio. The real guys. The Aerosmith guys. Steven Tyler and Joe Perry.

"We know how you feel about those lyrics," Jay told them. "Don't do the lyrics the way Steven done them. Do the lyrics the way Run and D would do them."

Run and D decided to come down. And so it began.

• • •

On that crisp Manhattan Sunday, an unusually large group assembled at Magic Venture Studios. Simmons and Rubin sat behind the board. Title-wise, they were technically equals, coproducers, although as time passed one would be recognized as the ultimate hip-hop impresario, the other as a kind of rock star whisperer.

There was a Beastie Boy or two, the producer's older brother, studio assistants, one of Rubin's buddies from NYU, a girlfriend, a drug-addled guitarist, the PR guy, journalists, photographers, and a frizzy-haired road manager named Lyor Cohen.

They were here to watch Run-DMC record a cover of Aerosmith's "Walk This Way." It was a remarkable idea for two reasons. There was nothing new about DJs using beats from mainstream rock songs. But Rubin wanted Run and D to do more than rhyme over that beat. They were supposed to do a cover version using Steven Tyler's lyrics. No rapper did that. What's more, Rubin had somehow finagled getting Tyler and Perry to come in and guest on the track.

Today, when genre-busting mash-ups are commonplace, when an aging Beatle can record with Kanye or Metallica will jam out with Lang Lang, this collaboration may not sound like the revolution. But just find a similar team-up before that Sunday in March. You can't. Before "Walk This Way," rock and rap were separated by a gulf as wide as the Pacific.

This revolution would be televised.

Tim Sommer, the musician and former college disc jockey who now worked at MTV, saw to that. At the twenty-four-hour video network, Sommer wasn't always taken seriously. Some of his colleagues, with their Starship and Thompson Twins videos, would snicker at his coverage ideas, particularly those that involved the notion that hip-hop had a future. But Sommer had one important supervisor's ear. Doug Herzog, a rising star at the network and the guy who oversaw the channel's small music news crew, knew that Timmy knew his stuff. So an MTV News crew arrived at Magic Venture.

There was also the *Spin* magazine associate editor Sue Cummings. She brought a photographer, as she planned to gather material for an upcoming cover story on Aerosmith. Years later, after Cummings had abandoned the business and moved west to Washington to work as a nurse practitioner, she would insist that she had, in fact, set this whole thing up. That's hard to believe, although it's easy to imagine she was part of the swirling brainstorm that led to the idea. Cummings and Sommer had dated. They were both friends with Rubin from their days at NYU.

The funny thing is how little the stars of the session seemed to understand what it could mean. Tyler and Perry were just glad they were getting paid to show up. They were scuffling, trying to both kick and feed their various habits, and this was a day off from their tour. Their Aerosmith bandmates were absent. Had they rejected the idea of working with rappers? Were they intentionally excluded? Maybe they just weren't needed. For now, nobody seemed to care.

"It really wasn't that big of a deal to us," said Perry. "Like this is a chance to give our career a boost or get black guys on MTV. We didn't even know if it was going to go on the record."

That there was so much coverage still bugged Run years

later. Hell, they were already stars. The last record, *King of Rock*, was a smash. They had most of *Raising Hell* done, and that record was hot. Why should it take a couple white boys to get everybody excited?

Run and D resisted even in the moment, goofing around in the booth, their improvised take on an Aerosmith classic captured by the MTV cameras, though most of the footage would be stuffed away in the archives and never aired. Run and D would actually have to rerecord their vocal tracks after not taking the first pass seriously enough.

Even with the studio packed, even with bona fide rock stars in that room, the moment felt more like what it wasn't than what it was. This was not a chance for the pairs to jump into the studio with one of their heroes. This wasn't Run and D hopping on the mic with Grandmaster Caz, or Jeff Beck joining Aerosmith to jam out on "Train Kept a Rollin'." This wasn't an all-star mash-up because there was no such thing as an all-star mash-up in 1986. To Run-DMC, it must have felt like homework.

History has a way of reshaping events. It marks serendipity as destiny, turns a snap of inspiration—Louis Armstrong peeling off the opening cadenza on "West End Blues," Elvis slapping down $3.98 to commit his quivering voice to acetate—into important chapters of the cultural canon.

Such is the case with "Walk This Way." Released on July 4, 1986, it became the first rap song played on mainstream rock radio and the genre's first Top 10 hit (actually, rising to number four) on the *Billboard* charts. The song would be included on so many lists: *Rolling Stone*'s greatest songs of all time, the Rock and Roll Hall of Fame's 500 Songs That Shaped Rock and Roll,

VH1's 100 Greatest Rock Songs. It would win both groups a Soul Train award.

In 1986, the song also served as an antidote to the slickness increasingly popular during the MTV generation. It introduced one group, Run-DMC, to a new crowd. It saved another.

As the money rolled in, a curious thing happened. "Walk This Way" made it safe to be black and mainstream. Years later, radio executives and MTV programmers still insisted that they found it offensive that anyone dared accuse them of racist programming practices in the 1980s. As their stories went, they were simply following a rock radio format, and that framework just happened to exclude rap from the airwaves. But pretending to be color-blind is naive, especially when one color, green, changed everything. Run-DMC's "Walk This Way" made millions, making it safe to bust the format. It also proved that hip-hop, dismissed by many as a fad, had legs.

At the end of May 1986, Tracy Marrow was one of the thousands of fans who packed the Los Angeles Memorial Sports Arena to see Run-DMC headline a show with LL Cool J on the bill. Marrow had been rapping for years as Ice-T, taking his name from the legendary pimp Iceberg Slim.

When he had seen Run-DMC in the past, they'd played clubs. The *Raising Hell* experience was altogether different.

"They had this laser show," said Marrow. "I was trying to rap, but I didn't realize it could be arena level. Up to that point, rap was something you did at house parties, garages, and basements. I had never seen production. They made me see that hip-hop was rock and roll in the sense you could play arenas with big speakers and lights. That shit was out. I think that night I went home and wrote."

"Walk This Way" would turn Run-DMC, already rap superstars, into music superstars. There would be bigger venues, magazine covers, and prime space on that great sonic billboard, MTV. For Aerosmith, the collaboration would do even more, relaunching a band thought dead by many into a revival that made them more popular than ever. For rap itself, "Walk This Way" represented the kind of historic marker that rock experienced when Elvis thrust his pelvis on *The Milton Berle Show* thirty years earlier.

Before "Walk" struck in 1986, hip-hop was a small underground community of independent labels and scrappy promoters. After "Walk," it became a nation, a genre that would soak itself into virtually every element of culture, from music and film to fashion and politics. If Frank Sinatra famously performed at the Nixon and Reagan White Houses, it is only fitting that during Barack Obama's tenure, Common visited 1600 Pennsylvania Avenue five times. And as the president prepared his final State of the Union Address, he tweeted a favorite Jay Z lyric.

"Walk This Way" was more than a Top 10 hit. It changed our culture.

Part One
BEFORE

Chapter 1
RUN-DMC: HOLLIS

It almost always begins with two. Keith and Mick. John and Paul. Chuck and Flav. They meet on a train, in a club, in homeroom. They realize they've got something in common, share a record, a rhyme, and a chorus, and they're off.

Years later, when it's all gone mad, when the mishegas of superstardom turns even the tightest brotherhood into a made-for-TV movie, that initial spark can be easy to forget. But it's always there, at the center, and it's why fans never stop longing for a reunion.

Start with Run, who put them together. And start in Hollis, where they met, and upstairs, where he first heard those sounds.

"Number one, there's the attic," he said.

Forty years later, Joseph Ward Simmons was a minister who liked everyone to call him Rev. Run. He lived in a mansion in Saddle River, New Jersey. He was shiny-bald, heavy, and wearing a black Adidas sweat suit.

Asked about growing up, though, he would snap straight back to the Me Decade, to Joey, that scrappy, basketball-playing kid with an Afro and dirty-dawg smile. And the attic.

Rev. Run wouldn't even drink Red Bull anymore. But when he closed his eyes, he could still smell the weed stench leaking out the door and down the stairs as his older brothers cranked up the radio.

There were three brothers in that house. Danny was the oldest, Russell in the middle, Joey the youngest. The Simmons family had moved into a three-bedroom brick house at 104-16 205th Street in 1965, when Joey was not yet one year old.

Daniel Simmons Sr. worked in the New York City schools as an attendance supervisor. He also participated in the civil rights movement. He marched on Washington in 1963 and taught a course on black history at Pace University. Evelyn, his wife, taught preschool and painted in her spare time.

They were close with their boys, but they couldn't control them.

Danny Simmons, eleven years older than Joey, got deep into drugs. Russell dabbled, favoring angel dust, cocaine, and weed. He also liked to toss around his gang credentials, telling anybody who asked about his start as a dealer and his street smarts. But he was no thug.

"Russell, like any other kid who did anything on the street, they like to glorify that shit," said Danny.

He continued.

"Russell sold a little weed for me. I would buy a pound of weed and give Russell a quarter pound. But our father had a bachelor's degree, our mother went to college. Russell was taken care of. The only thing Russell ever sold was a little weed and some cocoa leaf incense faking it was coke. He was in a neighborhood gang because every other kid was in a gang. I personally do not like to further that stereotype that all these kids came from nothing and music made them. What made them is our parents, who got jobs and woke us up in the morning to go to school. We had college funds."

If Russell at least dabbled in the life, Joey stayed firmly out. He watched what it did to Danny, who was hooked on heroin at one point.

"He saw it all," said Russell. "His own brother shot a lot of dope. I went through hell. He had a good father, a good mother, and he was able to escape. But you still got family out there, you still got friends. It's not that much peer pressure. It's not like you got to come out and join the game."

Hollis is a 525-acre, southeastern stretch of Queens. For Run-DMC, it is what Liverpool was to the Beatles, but something more. The Beatles left the Mersey behind, and years later, they weren't writing elegiac remembrances of hanging out on the docks or playing the Cavern Club. They moved on. Run-DMC, on the other hand, held up their home neighborhood as a source of pride, whether rolling past their boys with the radio blasting or celebrating "Christmas in Hollis" on record long after they could afford to leave it behind. It's no wonder the cover of their authorized autobiography, *Tougher Than Leather*, features a Janette Beckman photo of the guys—and their crew—standing outside in Hollis back in the day.

It wasn't Bel-Air or even Long Island, but it wasn't something to turn your nose up at. Hollis in the '70s was an urban oasis compared to the burned-out brick buildings of the Bronx. "Moving on up" was the operative phrase, taking its cue from the popular sitcom *The Jeffersons*. In Hollis, you had a fenced-in yard, a driveway, and your own walls. You could be safe, plan for college, and build a life. Which is not to say it was perfect. There was crime, there was dealing, there were times and corners you didn't want to be out on by yourself.

The local high school, in particular, did not inspire confidence. The Simmons brothers and Jay Mizell went to Andrew Jackson High School. (Darryl, who became DMC, did not; his parents sent him to Catholic school.) When the school shut down in the early 1990s, state officials noted that a "heroin factory" had been run out of the basement at one point. Its four-year graduation rate hovered around 30 percent.

For Joey—before he became Run—everything was about music and basketball. He loved shooting hoops down in the playgrounds. His connection to music began in the attic. The space first belonged to Danny. He and Russell sometimes let Joey come up. He stared at the nite-glow paint on the walls. The Gil Scott-Heron poster.

"And that's where I hear Frankie Crocker, in the attic," Run said. "The biggest DJ in the world and jammin' to that when they let me come up there."

Frankie Crocker. Amazing hair, almost heavy metal hair. You can see him in photos backstage with Barry White, just before Thanksgiving 1974, with that golden smile, neat tie, and those locks flowing over his shoulders. Two years later, he turned to an Afro and a white suit when his Heart and Soul Orchestra released a pair of albums on Casablanca Records, the label that also put out the Village People and Donna Summer.

Crocker ruled the airwaves on WBLS-FM, 107.5. He cruised the city in a flashy car or, more famously one night, rode a white stallion through the New York streets to make the grandest entrance at Studio 54. He was purely disco and would claim to hate rap, at least the rap that came later, stripped of the slap bass and four-on-the-floor beat. But Crocker's raps were famous, as much a model for the first-generation MCs as for the harder rhymes of Caz or the Funky 4+1. Because Crocker's rhymes weren't being heard only in nightclubs. They were blasting over the airwaves, bristling with confidence and cool where anybody could hear them.

"*Good evening New York,*" Frankie would say to open his show over a waterbed of R&B chords. "*This is the show that's bound to put more dips in your hips. More cut in your strut and more glide in your stride.*

"*If you don't dig it, you know you've got a hole in your soul.*

"*And you don't eat chicken on Sunday.*

"*Tall, tan, young, and fine. Anytime you want me, baby, reach out for me. I'm your guy. Just as good to you as it is for you.*"

And then a James Brown grunt.

"*Ha ha ha. You get so much with the Frankie Crocker touch. After all, how could you lose with the stuff I use.*"

Yes, Frankie Crocker was everywhere. Joey Simmons hustled down the block to 197th Street, cutting through a backstreet instead of the main drag, Hollis Avenue, so he wouldn't get hassled, to see his buddy Darryl McDaniels. They'd been friends since grade school. Then they went to another kid's house and the dial was set to WBLS.

"And it's the coolest echo chamber 'experience experience, experience,'" said Run. "'Frankie Crocker, Crocker, Crocker, the cool chief rocker, Frankie Crocker.'"

His head was spinning. Who was this Frankie Crocker? Then, one day, he begged Russell for a little brotherly guidance. He pointed to the radio.

"'How do I get to Frankie Crocker?' He said, 'It's so easy. Go to the end of the radio station and the second you turn it like you're trying to go back, WBLS will come up.' I'm fascinated. I'm the king. I now can create and listen to Frankie Crocker."

By then, Danny was out of the house. Russell was still there, but he'd left the attic to the kid, the kid who by that point knew how to tune his radio to 107.5. Rev. Run told the story:

"Then I hear in the streets, 'Your brother was at the party last night.' What?" A dramatic pause. "Russell was at a party last night? What is he doing? 'Your brother, I heard your brother got on the mic last night.' My brother got on the mic? What is this?"

The parties started in the parks in the early '70s. There were full bands playing until DJ Kool Herc, in the Bronx and a good twenty-five-minute drive away from the Simmons kids, came around with two turntables and big-ass speakers he'd haul around in his convertible. They say Herc held the first hip-hop party in the common room at 1520 Sedgwick Avenue, in the Bronx, on August 11, 1973. A copy of the original invite is in a case at the Smithsonian. But what came next shaped the scene more dramatically, when the turntables came off the streets into the clubs.

And by the time Joey was old enough to get into an R-rated movie, what mattered is that Russell had moved onto the circuit. He even had a name for his company, Rush. And when he'd get back to 205th street, early morning, the kid would be waiting.

"I'd see him walk through the door with a guy named Kurtis Walker. Kurtis Blow. I did my job here when I'd hear him coming in at five, six in the morning. Immediately go cook breakfast. They're hungry. They probably got the munchies. I got to cook breakfast. Make sure Russell get those socks, that I didn't use up all the tube socks out of the basement. Cook breakfast to keep my brother happy. Bacon and eggs."

Kurt and Russell would be eating and the kid would be thinking about "Rush, a force in college parties," and he'd be asking, What can I do?

• • •

Son of Byford, brother of Al
Banna's my mamma and Run's my pal
It's McDaniels, not McDonald's

That was Darryl. He'd soon be the closer, the Devastating Mic Controller, the KHIIIINNNGGGG.

But back then he was the braniac, the kid with all A's, a crazy comic book collection, and a painful curfew. He was at home, getting antsy, listening to the other kids outside until ten, eleven, midnight.

"I'm hearing them laugh and do water guns all through the night," said DMC. "I was jealous, but I wasn't disappointed. I was really big with G.I. Joe, Evil Knievel. And the crazy thing with me is, I didn't just play with my dolls. I did movies with them."

What DMC didn't know then—he wouldn't find out until his thirties—was that he hadn't actually been born in Hollis. He was from Harlem, given up as a baby by his birth mother. This information would throw him into a deep depression, but ultimately help him understand who he was. Back then though, everything began and ended in Hollis.

To a comic book kid like Darryl, Queens had a mystique. Remember, Peter Parker's from Queens.

"The first time I saw the Roosevelt Island Tram, I almost suffocated. I'm in the car with my mother and father. I'm in the backseat and we're going over the 59th Street Bridge, my father's turning around. 'What the hell is wrong with the boy?' My mother, she's a nurse, she's turning around. 'What's wrong with you?' All I can think is, 'It does exist.' The first time I saw Roosevelt on a train was in *Spider-Man*. Or the Pan Am Building on Park Avenue. It's a classic shot."

The McDaniels' house ran to the rhythms of a time clock.

Darryl's parents were up early, with Byford working for the Metropolitan Transportation Authority as a station agent, and Banna as a nursing coordinator at a local hospital. Older brother, Alfred, also dug the comic books, a key to Darryl's embrace of fantasy. Is it any wonder the man who rapped that he was "Son of Byford," who gave himself a superhero name, studied Thor, Son of Odin?

Alfred is the one who picked up tapes on the street, the homemade hip-hop tapes you couldn't buy in stores. He also picked up a turntable, which the brothers put in the basement and linked to his mother's wood-cased record player.

"Me and my brother, we went out, bought a fifty-dollar mixer, this Gemini mixer, this silver mixer, about the size of a shoe box," said DMC. "The thing didn't even have a crossfade. Crossfade wasn't invented yet. The turntable we had didn't even match the turntable to my mother's system. But that's how bad we wanted the turntables. So it was just a makeshift system. I didn't have an amp, but it was good enough to allow me to be Grandmaster Flash."

D was cagey about the equipment at first. When his friend Run first asked him about it, he told him it was his brother's.

"Hip-hop was my personal thing," he said. "Like how I had my comic books. I would wake up in the morning and I would go DJ before I would go outside and hang with Joe and Ray and our whole crew. So nobody knew for a long time, and then what had happened was I used to do tapes."

One day, DMC made a tape rhyming over the Incredible Bongo Band's version of "Apache," a Kool Herc favorite, and played it for his buddies.

"And Joe was like, 'Yo, that's you, Darryl?' And I was like, 'Yeah.' And he didn't say nothing. And then ever so slowly, when he started coming to my house, I started to reveal. Like, he knew I could DJ, but slowly over time, like, we would be in the alleyway around the corner from my house where we used to hang out at. And my man, Douglas Hayes, who was my best friend growing up. He would start beating on the wall or on a table or a box or something. And I would just start saying rhymes that I was writing, and Joe would give me this look, 'Oh shit.'"

Run remembered the sense of wonder he felt when he discovered the turntables in the basement of 197th Street.

"I didn't know what that was about," he said. "He knew how to DJ. And he would DJ 'Super Sporm,' a record called 'Scratching It,' and records like that. Maybe even 'Walk This Way' was in the basement. I don't know at that time. It probably was. They had a nice little case of records. Taught me how to DJ.

Wow, Darryl's got DJ equipment. He's like a billionaire in my mind. I don't even know about it. You got it, in your basement, with a Gemini mixer. What is this?"

When he started writing rhymes, Darryl started like everybody else. He knew DJ Hollywood, the first king really, and the way he laid his voice over a dance beat. He'd be listening to Eddie Cheba on WFUV playing "Rapper's Delight" or Crocker's hipster jive. That stuff didn't quite hit him. Too slick, that "Hip hop, da hippy-hippy hop, have you ever been over your friend's house to eat and the food is gross?" kind of thing. This was not B-boy material. This was disco with an MC.

But then, high school. Joey Simmons headed to Andrew Jackson like his older brothers. Darryl got out, taking three trains and two buses to get to the private Rice High School, all boys and Catholic, on 125th and Lenox. You couldn't wear sneakers and jeans. But you could hear the new sound. Forget the softies in the Sugarhill Gang. Sundance from Afrika Bambaataa's Zulu Nation was in his class. DJ Red Alert did their prom.

"When I got to Rice, I started hearing Funky 4+1. Talking about 'I go to McDonald's / I got my sneakers on.' Over breakbeats and echo chambers. My style. 'My name is DMC-C-C-C. All-time great-great-great.' I got that from a girl."

That was Sharon Green, known as Sha-Rock in the Funky 4+1. They were one of the earliest crews and major innovators who, in 1981, were the first hip-hop group to play *Saturday Night Live* when Blondie brought them on. But it was early on, probably late 1977, that Sha-Rock remembered the group's manager, Jazzy Dee, investing in an echo chamber.

"Because females had started coming up behind me and every group would try to have a female with the same formula," said Sha-Rock. "We wanted to separate ourselves. Every time I'd say a rhyme, my manager knew exactly when to put the echo on to only allow certain words to be echoed. That allowed me to be separated from any MC and all MCs at that time until people realized what we were using."

DMC might have had the turntables. But he wasn't cooking bacon for Kurtis Blow and getting firsthand accounts of what went on in the clubs.

He also didn't have anybody to help him get out of the basement, at least right away. Joey did. Joey had Kurtis Blow. Kurtis gave him his first real break.

"He couldn't get into the clubs, so his thing was block parties and park jams," Blow remembered. "And he got a little reputation by getting on the mic a couple of times and really doing well, and so I took him under my wing."

Joey also got his own turntables and started to get fast—fast enough to acquire a stage name. DJ Run. When Kurtis Blow started getting big, making records, synching on *Soul Train*, he needed a DJ to back him up when he toured. Russell Simmons knew just who to bring in. His kid brother. Run got a pair of Quanta turntables and a mixer. Then he spent every minute up in the attic, practicing with a box of records. Eventually, DJ Run got yet another moniker: Son of Kurtis Blow.

"I put him against anybody," said Blow. "He actually was really fast. When he showed me how fast he was I immediately said, 'Oh, you've got to DJ for me.' That was around 1979. I was doing shows around the New York area, and then I got to do a show in New Jersey. We started going around. Going on flights. To Alabama. Texas. 1980 rolled around. I made 'The Breaks.'"

Then, one afternoon, Blow showed up at the Simmons' house and noticed something worrisome for a rapper about to go out on tour. His DJ had a cast on his right arm. Run had been playing basketball over at the church with Darryl. He broke his wrist.

"Don't worry about it, I'll still DJ," Joey told Blow, promising he could do it with one arm.

A one-armed DJ. No thanks.

That's how Blow saw it. Years later, he would say that injury inadvertently led to the creation of hip-hop's first and most important supergroup. But it's hard to imagine it wasn't just a matter of time.

The pieces were already in place.

The older brother to manage. The boyhood friend to rhyme beside him onstage. The producer was also in pocket. That was Larry Smith. The bassist and veteran backing musician had been helping produce Blow.

So the kid in the cast would not hit the road. Blow hired David Reeves, later to be known as Davy DMX, to serve as DJ. It made perfect sense.

"I was good, but Davy was definitely better," said Rev. Run years later. "So Davy went on to be with Kurt. I got with Darryl."

• • •

DJ Run's transformation into MC Run began with a couple of false starts. Trevor Gale, a drummer who had already earned praise for his work with Nona Hendryx, wrote a song called

"Street Kid" for the kid to rap over. They recorded it, but Gale couldn't sell the demo.

"Action" was a different story. The song emerged out of Smith's need for a group to back Blow and anybody else he produced on club dates. He recruited Gale and Reeves and christened them Orange Krush. In 1981, they went into the studio to record a single.

"Action" is not a musical masterpiece. The worst element is actually Russell Simmons. He's on vocals, with the tape sped up to turn his voice into that of a helium-sucking Smurf. The bass and guitar is pure disco. And the chorus is sung by Alyson Williams, who would have a string of R&B hits later in the 1980s. What matters about "Action," what makes it important, is Gale's beat.

They couldn't use a drum machine, even though they wanted to. Advertisements for Oberheim's new creation, the DMX, were just starting to appear in specialty recording magazines in late 1981. It's unlikely the DMX was even available for purchase at the moment Smith was laying down "Action." But even if it was, the first machines would have been far too expensive for a group without a record contract. The DMX listed for close to $3,000.

So Smith came up with an alternative. A human drum machine. That would be Gale.

Gale remembered the strangeness of the moment.

"You're a real musician, you're into Led Zeppelin and Jimi Hendrix and Chicago and Blood Sweat and Tears and James Brown and Kool and the Gang, then somebody comes along and said, 'You're going to play rap.' What? After I started rehearsals, I started understanding it was like being a spaceman and being John Glenn orbiting the Earth in a little capsule. Something brand-new and something so improvisational, the stuff that Davy was doing on the turntables, it was like, this is crazy."

Smith sat in the control room. Gale sat at his kit in the studio, a rhythm box keeping time. There was no music. "He said, 'Play against that.' Play against what? 'Just play.' He's yelling through the glass. So I played."

"That beat," remembered Akili Walker, the producer who worked with Smith, "was dope."

It also wouldn't die with Orange Krush, which Smith had to disband when he ran out of money. Gale's beat would become a key element when Smith started recording this new rap group Run-DMC. By then, he had a DMX machine. He programmed the beat and gave it a name, Krush Groove. And then he applied that beat to the music. There would be four Krush Grooves in Run-DMC's catalog, starting with "Sucker M.C.'s (Krush-Groove 1)" through to "Together Forever (Krush-Groove 4) (Live at Hollis Park '84)."

But there's also an important piece of "Action" that didn't make the vinyl cut. DJ Run's rap. Decades later he could still remember the words.

Undercover lover, the master spy.
Used to work for the FBI.

"Whatever I said, it was really good," he remembered.

Was he upset when he got edited out? Did he feel like he'd missed his big chance?

"I don't think I was destroyed," Run said. "I just loved rapping."

He would get his real chance soon enough. Run was sitting on the couch with DMC one day when Russell came home. Maybe Spoonie Gee was with him. "Kick that rhyme, Joe," one of them said. He did, and then he looked over at his friend. "D can rhyme, too," he told them.

"Darryl, with those glasses?" Russell was laughing. "He looks like Preach from *Cooley High*."

That was true. But that didn't have a thing to do with making a record.

"I'm not making no demo without Darryl," Run told his brother.

It was a reminder that leverage, sometimes, is not about money or fame or what you can threaten. Sometimes, it's just about being loyal to your buddy sitting next to you on the couch.

Chapter 2

AEROSMITH: TOXIC TWINS

They were never brothers, no matter what you heard. They shared a band, a Blue Army, drugs, a few scuba dives in Hawaii, but not much else. You don't need an advanced degree in psychology to tell the difference between these two men. Just talk to them for a split second.

Steven Tyler blasts into a conversation. He makes up words and phrases and draws on entire waiting rooms of personalities. He dances across decades, cities, and relationships. He can pluck out a moment from the Nixon era that's as raw and ragged as something that happened yesterday. He's also not afraid to reveal the truth, at least the truth he believes to be right, even if it reflects badly on his record company, his bandmates, and most often, himself. Emotions are not secrets to be bottled up or cordoned off by high-powered publicists. Emotions are meant to be shared. "You know, man, I was brought up Italian," he'll eventually shout by way of explanation.

Joe Perry has his personality knob set on permanent mumble. Don't misinterpret that. He's not incoherent or disinterested. It's about being shy, withdrawn, and stoic. He's also Italian—his mother's side—which proves that heritage has nothing to do with this.

"Joe was never a rock star," said Jack Douglas, who produced Aerosmith's greatest work in the 1970s. "He was a bookish nerd who picked up a guitar. He is not a public person, not a natural performer. Steven is the real deal. He's a rock and roll animal. If he wasn't a rock and roll animal now, he would have been in vaudeville. He's a showman. And he's talented. He's musically talented, he's got a great voice, he's got all the goods, and he saw in Joe the guy that could be his brother, and he tried to form that and make that, make him the Keith Richards to his Mick Jagger. But it wasn't ever to be."

Actually, you could argue that Tyler and Perry ended up very much like Keith and Mick. The Stones front men were also promoted as brothers, while in truth they were as likely to sleep with each other's girlfriends as share a spot of tea. They bickered, formed alliances, worked as much on their own as together. And in that space, that universe of ultracompetitive chaos, they found just the right balance of tension and affection to create a vital slice of the rock canon for a decade or more, depending on whether you call the last great Rolling Stones record *Sticky Fingers*, *Exile on Main St.*, or, god forbid, *Bridges to Babylon*. When you consider how difficult it is to keep a musical brotherhood together—think of Page and Plant, John and Paul, or actual blood brothers Ray and Dave Davies—it's quite admirable that after forty-five years, Tyler and Perry are still part of the same band. Not that it was ever going to be easy.

"You want those guys to be clicking and really out together and not at each other's throats," said Tom Hamilton, Aerosmith's bassist. "That's kind of the story of the band. We have periods where things are great and periods where things are just a disaster."

Joe Perry did not get emotional when he talked about Tyler. He did refer to him as a brother, but with a qualifier.

"I met guys who don't even talk to their brothers, and there's others that are, like, joined at the hip," said Perry.

He paused.

"When I was about fourteen, my mother had a baby," he said. "And he had a bad heart and he died after five days in the hospital. I love my sister, but it would have been cool to have a brother. Maybe that's a subconscious thing that's always been there. Steven and I definitely have some kind of connection. Even though we might be a thousand miles apart, he's like a brother."

They found each other the same way most bands do. Geography.

Aerosmith would become famous as the Bad Boys from Boston, but it would've been more accurate to call them the Gang from the Granite State. That's where they met, in New Hampshire, in 1969.

Steven Tallarico grew up in the Bronx. Music coursed through his family. His paternal grandfather, Giovanni, was an Italian immigrant who played cello. His father, Victor, studied piano at Juilliard and later performed at country clubs, as well as giving lessons. The boy's first experience with music came huddled under the Steinway grand, which somehow fit in the tiny apartment, listening to Victor play Chopin, Bach, and Beethoven. This was a loving childhood, but not a quiet one. Mother, father, sister, aunts, uncles . . . all around the table, yelling. "They argued a lot," Tyler said. "They expressed their feelings.

That's how I was. A very touchy-feely, loving guy that was a sorcerer of melody."

When he was thirteen, Tyler stumbled upon a drum set in a friend's basement and started pounding. He fell in love. Before long, he'd be taking lessons and playing covers with his band the Strangers.

Joe Perry grew up in Massachusetts. His father, Tony Pereira, was an accountant. His mother, Mary, earned a master's degree in physical education and headed the gym department in the local high school. The boy, Anthony Joseph, loved reading, the woods, and dreamed of being a deep-sea diver. He even had his parents drive him into Boston to hear explorer Jacques Cousteau lecture. But Perry found school difficult, even baffling. Later, they would have a name and a treatment for it: ADHD. Back then, a kid was left to struggle, to wonder why a book he read on Tuesday would be forgotten by Wednesday. Perry eventually went to a private prep school, Vermont Academy, but he never finished. They say he got kicked out for growing his hair long. Perhaps. But his grades were no good and he'd lost his confidence. By that point, Perry had heard Jeff Beck and Jimi Hendrix and decided he needed a Les Paul. He couldn't afford one yet, though, and settled for the Silvertone his parents bought him at Sears.

Perry had always spent his summers diving and hiking at the family summer home on Lake Sunapee, New Hampshire. He formed the Jam Band there, a trio with drummer Dave "Pudge" Scott and Tom Hamilton on bass. And that's where, during the summer of 1969, he met Steven Tyler.

Tyler had been playing in Chain Reaction, a band that had recorded a pair of singles and opened for the Yardbirds, the Byrds, and the Beach Boys. He caught Perry's band playing at a local spot, the Barn, and would eventually jam with him in New Hampshire, singing and sitting in on drums. He told Perry they should think about forming a band.

But Perry and Hamilton were going to Boston, they told him, believing they needed to be in the city if they really wanted to go professional. In September 1970, the pair moved there and soon met drummer Joey Kramer, who was studying at the Berklee College of Music. Kramer had his own baggage. He had grown up with an abusive father, his arms often covered in bruises. He loved music, caught The Beatles on Ed Sullivan, but it wasn't Ringo that got him to pick up his sticks. It was the desire for the camaraderie, the bond, he imagined came with a band.

"That was always my biggest problem," said Kramer. "I always wanted everybody to get along and be brothers and be friends and have a good time together and take over the world. It wasn't hardly about the music. It was about being in a gang."

In Boston, Perry got in touch with Tyler and asked if he wanted in. *Steven Tallarico.* It turned out that Kramer had known him in high school. Steven was the badass who had once showed up at a friend's basement with a Hendrix record.

Tyler said he would come to Boston, but he insisted on bringing a friend, Ray Tabano, to serve as the second guitarist. Tabano wasn't much of a player, and before long he would be out, replaced by another Berklee kid, Brad Whitford. It was 1970, and there was now a band named Aerosmith.

Years later, the five of them would return as heroes to 1325 Commonwealth Avenue in the Brighton section of Boston. Standing on a platform, they blasted through nine songs in front of thirty thousand people at a giant block party meant to commemorate their beginnings. But 1970 was anything but glamorous. Tyler and Kramer shared a room. Hamilton slept on the couch. Perry and Mark Lehman, a friend who worked as a crew member, lived in one of the other rooms.

"In the beginning with the band, I told them I think we should get an apartment and live together," said Tyler. "That way we'll wind up writing songs. We won't leave each other's sides. We can jam and play, and my dream came true. We got 1325 Comm. Ave., and one day, three months in, Joe Perry was sitting on our tour manager's waterbed and we came up with 'Movin' Out.' This band, we made a pact. Like blood brothers. We said we're going to stay here until we die."

The funny thing is that Tyler explained this with more than a pinch of sadness and regret. As he looked back, he saw them, from the start, treating him as the outsider, "an alien."

"If I got some blow, I would tap the gram out on the table," Tyler said. "If those guys got blow, then they'd hide it from me."

It got worse as they grew older.

Tyler was the emotional, loving, temperamental, demanding, desperate front man in one corner. The guys were growing older, getting married, settling down, in the other.

Perry and Tyler went from 1325 to another apartment, but that didn't last. The guitarist had found himself a girl. He decided to move out. Tyler did not take well to this.

"When Joe had women in his life," said Tim Collins, the band's former manager, "Steven always wanted them to be secondary to their relationship. Because the two of them, basically, their songs were their children. I don't think it was any sexual thing, but it was an emotional love affair for Steven and not so much for Joe."

Did it hurt his feelings? Ask Tyler now and he references Elissa Jerret, once a childhood friend and eventually a rival. She had met Perry in those New Hampshire days, they got together and embarked on a stormy seven-year marriage. Tyler remembered that moment, in the '70s, when he told them he felt excluded from their relationship.

"And when I told them how I felt, they laughed and walked away," he said. "That's when I wrote 'Sweet Emotion.'"

He quotes the song.

"'Talk about things that nobody cares / You're wearing out things nobody wears.' She had just gotten back from England and Joe was smitten and he left the apartment. I went, 'Jesus, we just fucking wrote a song together.'"

"It was a highly charged relationship," said Perry. "That moment was the culmination of months of maybe hearing that, because I have a relationship, I'm not in the band. I'm like, 'Wait a second,' he's off fucking girls and then he got married and all that stuff. And I'm there for the band. Everybody will tell you."

There was also, for Tyler, a sense of isolation. That he would always be the one on the outside. At band meetings, he grew so accustomed to having his ideas squashed that he began to use reverse psychology. He would suggest what he *didn't* want. They'd disagree and he'd get his way.

He returned to the moment Perry decided to move out of the apartment.

"If I said, 'I want you the fuck out of this house. Why don't you move in with her? I want to stay here myself.'"

He laughed.

"He might have stayed."

It was more than complicated when the others entered the discussion. They complained about Tyler, about LSD—lead singer disease—and they snickered when he split with the band's management and, after a concert in 2009, spoke of making a solo record and looking out for "brand Tyler." They slagged on that solo debut, a country-tinged record that finally came out in 2016, and seemed to take pleasure when it didn't turn into a smash.

But they also conceded that, even with his hang-ups and blowups, there's a transparency with Steven, the idea that you don't need a cryptographist to interpret his emotional state. With Steven, you always know where you stand. That's not Joe Perry.

"I'll tell you this much about Joe," said Kramer. "Joe is a difficult guy to get to know. He's painfully shy. During the first week that the band was together, Joe and I were walking down Newbury Street by ourselves and I looked at him and said, 'Wow, man, this is really fucking great. We got a fucking band together, we're going to be pals. Everything is going to be great. We're going to make great music. I'm just so excited.' Joe turned to me and he said, 'Why do we have to be friends to play in a band together?'

"Mind you, this is fucking fifty years later and that sentence that he said still sticks in my mind."

• • •

They were far from an overnight success. Aerosmith's self-titled debut, recorded in 1972, had glimmers of what was to come—Tyler's screeching finale on "One Way Street," the epic power ballad "Dream On"—but so much of that record merely filled space. The strangest element may have been Tyler's voice. He's all throat, singing, as he put it later, like Kermit the Frog. Not that anybody noticed. *Rolling Stone* didn't even review the record.

Things would be different the next time around. That's when Jack Douglas arrived.

Douglas was a native New Yorker and Beatles freak who had started at the lowest of levels—janitor—when he began working at the Record Plant in New York during the late 1960s. He had a knack for being in the right place at the right time. During the summer of 1971, that found him working in the tape library in a back room when John Lennon wandered in. The recovering Beatle seemed desperate to get away, if only for a few minutes, from the increasingly unhinged Phil Spector during the recording of what would become his second solo album, *Imagine*. He took a liking to the kid and brought him into the main recording studio. Douglas would eventually get an engineering credit.

By the time Douglas started working with Aerosmith, late in 1973, he had engineered Alice Cooper's *Billion Dollar Babies* and become the de facto producer of the New York Dolls' stunning debut after Todd Rundgren got fed up trying to corral the band.

Bob Ezrin, Alice Cooper's producer, considered taking the Aerosmith job, but his schedule was packed. He also wondered whether his strong personality would create too much friction with Tyler. He suggested the more mild-mannered Douglas, his sometime engineer, for the job.

From the start, Douglas could tell the band had great ideas and that they had grown remarkably since their first sessions. That's what months on the road opening for the Dolls, Mott the Hoople, and the Kinks can do. The material they brought to the studio for their second album was far better than the songs on their debut.

Tyler had "Seasons of Wither" and "Lord of the Thighs," songs with dynamic shifts in mood and instrumentation. He and Perry wrote "Same Old Song and Dance," a rocker with one of the guitarist's signature riffs. They also planned to record one of their favorite covers, the show-closing, blues standard "Train Kept a Rollin'" that they had first heard by the Yardbirds.

But in preproduction, Douglas came to a realization. Perry and Whitford were good, but not good enough. He needed some outside help on guitars.

"They weren't where they wanted to be," he said. "They wanted to be more than a local band from Boston where everybody in the band kind of plays okay. They wanted to be at a higher level. They wanted to compete with big bands. Led Zeppelin. They wanted to be up there, and they couldn't with the way they played at that point."

It wasn't chops or speed. They didn't need a shredder. They needed something harder to define, the sort of expressive guitar playing that comes through experience. Douglas knew just the guys for the job. Guitarists Steve Hunter and Dick Wagner had played on *Billion Dollar Babies* and Lou Reed's *Berlin*.

"I remember that I got Steven and Brad and Joe into a room and I said, 'Listen, we're going to try this. It'll make the record better,'" remembered Douglas. "Brad was like, uh, he was a little bit more passive about it. Joe was angry. Steven was like, 'Yes, that's a great idea.'"

The proof is in the playing on *Get Your Wings*, which was released on March 1, 1974. Wagner's melodic solo opens "Same Old Song and Dance" and cuts through the verses, playing off Michael Brecker's saxophone. Hunter blasts into "Train Kept a Rollin'," and the pair split the solos throughout the closing of "Train." For years, everybody kept the secret. It was easy. Live, Perry and Whitford played the solos note for note.

"The deal I had with Dick and Steve was that when I did this whole thing, I said, it comes with no credit and some lessons." Douglas laughed.

Perry didn't remember any lessons. He did remember what he picked up from watching what equipment the duo used.

"They had these amazing-sounding Fender combos, amps, and that really helped when I started using them in the studio," he said.

By now, he and Whitford were, he said, "sponges." One night, they were opening for the New York Dolls at Max's Kansas City and watching Johnny Thunders, that unpredictable way he attacked the notes, that dangerous who-gives-a-shit genius that worked so well until the junkie took over and the who-gives-a-shit genius broke down and brought the gig to a grinding halt. They would also be in the wings, in Chicago, as Mahavishnu John McLaughlin dazzled the audience.

"It's almost like a slingshot," said Perry. "You let go of the slingshot and the pocket picks up speed when you let go. We were hitting the road and playing with a lot of different bands. We went from being just fans in the audience to being fans onstage."

It was perfect timing. When Aerosmith came off the road after touring behind *Get Your Wings*, Perry and Whitford were completely different players.

They also had something special to share with their producer. It was a riff Perry had worked up during a sound check in Hawaii.

Chapter 3

RUN-DMC: LARRY SMITH, KURT, AND THE FEVER

You didn't need four stars in *Rolling Stone* or Casey Kasem's imprimatur. Larry Smith had a special way of providing, ahem, feedback. There he was, behind the board, laughing his ass off, and he'd jump up, shout, and grab his crotch.

"It's banging. My dick is hard. I see the mailman."

Jalil Hutchins, Whodini's front man, laughed as he remembered his producer's favorite lines. He could still hear the voice and slips into Larryspeak, a kind of goofy growl as he tells this story.

The mailman?

"That means the mailman got the check," said Hutchins, and paused. "It's crazy, waiting for a grown man to hold his shit."

You can talk all you want about superproducers. George Martin, Rick Rubin, T Bone Burnett. Just keep this in mind: From 1984 to 1987, Larry Smith oversaw six records—three by Whodini, two by Run-DMC, and the debut of the Fat Boys—that sold millions of copies. That's Phil Spector territory. And while Phil Spector got rich, famous, creepy, and yet somehow kept getting gigs during his long, steady decline—the man was still producing while on trial for a murder he would be convicted of—Larry Smith disappeared.

He was in England, working on Whodini's *Open Sesame*, when Rick Rubin came into the studio to produce Run-DMC's third album, *Raising Hell*. That Whodini record, released in May 1987, would be Smith's last gold record. By 1988, he was a ghost. He was working on Christian music and a Billy Preston Christmas album around 2006. Then, in late 2007, he had his first stroke. The second left him unable to talk. When Smith died, at a rehab center in 2014, it was in relative anonymity.

This abrupt fall pains DMC. On a day years later in New York, when he was supposed to be talking about his self-help memoir, he was asked about Smith. It seemed wrong, he was told, that the producer had been virtually wiped clean of hip-hop's history hard drive.

"There's no *Raising Hell* if it wasn't for Larry Smith," he said, banging his fist on the table. "I told his son, 'Your father is the greatest hip-hop producer nobody knows about. That's his title. That's the movie, that's the book. You make sure you let the world know about your father.'"

The truth is, Larry Smith never dreamed of being the greatest hip-hop anything of all time.

"I never wanted to be a fucking producer," his official bio read in the mid-'80s. "I like playing in a band!"

Smith grew up in St. Albans, only a short walk from the Hollis neighborhood where the Simmons family lived. He was thirteen years older than Joey and went to Andrew Jackson High School with the oldest Simmons brother, Danny. There was something else the two families had in common. They grew up comfortably.

Larry's father, Nathan, owned a dry cleaner's on Linden

Boulevard. His brother, Robert, was a high school basketball star who everybody called Monkey because, at six foot six, he could play. As a boy, Larry remembered hearing the blues records his mother listened to as she did housework. Later, at Andrew Jackson High, he got to be friends with an older kid, Robert Ford. They'd go to concerts together: the Grateful Dead at the Fillmore East, the Chambers Brothers, early Earth, Wind & Fire.

Larry played bass, and when one of his bands had a gig, Ford would help haul the Hammond B3 organ up the stairs.

"You have to go through so much work just to make one note," Nathan Smith would say, laughing.

There were the March Saints and the Brighter Side of Darkness. There was also Val Burke, who played bass for Willie Feaster and the Mighty Magnificents. Smith would call him his mentor. For years, Burke's group recorded for All Platinum, a record label whose signature act, the Moments, hit number three with 1970's "Love on a Two-Way Street." Sylvia and Joe Robinson owned the label. Remember those two. When All Platinum bottomed out in the late 1970s, they founded Sugar Hill Records.

Smith got his first taste of the studio in 1967, while still in high school, playing with a local group called the Firebolts. He moved to Chicago in 1972, back to New York City the next year, to Albany in 1976 and, finally, to Toronto in 1978, where he served as the bandleader for a musical called *Indigo*. He also spent long periods of time on the road, backing other musicians.

Ford remembered seeing Smith once, in Kansas City, around 1977, when they were both passing through. By then, Ford was working in the production department at *Billboard* magazine and writing reviews on the side. And on that beat, Ford wrote two of the earliest stories about the developing hip-hop scene. They weren't exactly blockbusters. "B-Beats Bombarding Bronx" ran on page 65 on July 1, 1978. It found Ford at Downstairs Records, reporting on the curious demand for obscure R&B cutouts like the Incredible Bongo Band's "Bongo Rock."

"The requests, for the most part, come from young black disco DJs from the Bronx who are buying the records just to play the 30 seconds or so of rhythm breaks that each disk contains," Ford wrote.

A year later, on May 1, 1979, Ford landed on page 3 with a short piece on the other development on the club scene, the "Jive Talking N.Y. DJs Rapping Away in Black Discos."

He wrote of the biggest star, DJ Hollywood, playing the Apollo, his tapes a hot commodity on the streets. He also referenced other masters-of-ceremony, DJs Eddie Cheba, Lovebug Starski, and Kurtis Blow, a community college kid who "hopes disco will be a springboard into broadcasting."

Then "Rapper's Delight" arrived in September on the Robinsons' new label.

• • •

If the Sugarhill Gang seemed to come out of nowhere, it's because they did. Instead of plucking a group of ready-made MCs out of a club—Grandmaster Caz, Hollywood, the Funky 4+1—Sylvia and Joe Robinson manufactured the hip-hop equivalent of the Monkees.

The Robinsons certainly knew what they were doing. Sylvia

had been a hit maker herself as far back as the 1950s as one half of Mickey & Sylvia and had a number three song in 1973 with her solo turn on "Pillow Talk." But business had slowed until, in 1979, the Robinsons founded Sugar Hill, named after the affluent neighborhood that emerged during the Harlem Renaissance a half century earlier.

Sugar Hill Records was not like anybody else. They were in New Jersey, for one thing.

The label got started after Sylvia's son brought her to a club to hear an MC for the first time. She was stunned by what she heard and saw. It was electric. Rather than hire an already established group, she decided to put together her own and name it after the new label. The Robinsons found two MCs and a pizza guy, who pretended to be an MC, working near them in New Jersey. They hired a band of seasoned studio musicians to rerecord the music on Chic's number one hit "Good Times." They pushed out the record on September 16, 1979, and watched, in delight, as "Rapper's Delight" became a smash.

Years later, the real rappers would say they hated it. That shit was softer than a bag of rotten tomatoes. They would resent the money that flowed to Sugar Hill, and they would resent the way the Robinsons refused to share the wealth. But in the moment, the main response to "Rapper's Delight" was shock. It didn't make sense. The music was meant to be live, mashed together by a DJ, responding to the kids on the dance floor. Nobody had really considered hip-hop a viable recorded product.

The Robinsons, for all their faults, saw past that. They understood that the rules in hip-hop were far from established. The very nature of the performance called for appropriating other people's music. They didn't hesitate to do the same on record.

In rock, stealing or borrowing a tune would get you sued. That's how Willie Dixon got his name on Led Zeppelin's 1969 Top 10 single "Whole Lotta Love," and how George Harrison spent years in court, until a judge eventually decided he subconsciously swiped from the 1962 girl group hit "He's So Fine" for "My Sweet Lord," released eight years later.

In rap, the rules weren't necessarily different, but the commercial expectations were so low that nobody bothered to go by the book. Actually, there was no book. And the Robinsons weren't the type to try to get ahead of the copyright curve. Why the house band? Professional samplers like the Akai S900 wouldn't come out until 1986. And they didn't need to waste time messing with tape loops. Instead, they got top studio musicians to re-create the sound they wanted and then laid those lines over it. That's how "Good Times" ended up as the backing track for "Rapper's Delight."

Then there was the matter of their MCs. Michael "Wonder Mike" Wright and Guy "Master Gee" O'Brien, two of the recruits, could work the mic. Henry Jackson understood a lot more about making pepperoni pizzas than about flow on the mic. He had no rhymes, but he did know somebody whose rhyme books were overflowing. Jackson worked in some service capacity—security or management—for one of the great MCs of the day, Curtis Brown, then known as Casanova Fly and later Grandmaster Caz. Brown found it funny when Jackson approached him one day and told him that the Robinsons wanted him to rap.

"I said: 'For what? You don't rap,'" said Brown. "'You ain't no MC. Didn't you tell them about me?' He's like, 'The lady heard my tapes and she likes my voice.' So anyway. He said, 'I need you to write me some rhymes because we going in the studio.' I'm not thinking nothing of it. I'm not thinking this is going anywhere. So I'm like: 'Cool. Come over my house.' He came to my house. I threw a bunch of rhymes on the table and said, 'Say this, say this, and say that.'"

Brown kept meticulous rhyme books. There is a reason, years later, why Cornell University would acquire them for their rare library, stored alongside an original copy of the Gettysburg Address. Film director Charlie Ahearn, who would feature the MC prominently in 1982's *Wild Style*, remembered visiting Brown's place in the Bronx and seeing the stacks of lyrics.

"And he just laid out these books on his bed and opened them up and each page had the lyrics to a rap and they were done in the most impeccable penmanship, without a mistake," said Ahearn. "This guy wasn't, like, working on this stuff. This was the preservation of raps that he had written."

If there is rap jail, and not the one currently occupied by Iggy Azalea, it should be reserved for the cheaters and hucksters who took what wasn't theirs. And nobody stole more than Sugar Hill. The Robinsons were audacious enough to grab the music from a number one hit, Chic's "Good Times," without giving credit. Only after the release, under pressure from Chic's Nile Rodgers and Bernard Edwards, did Sugar Hill list the duo as co-songwriters and pay them. Caz was not so lucky. That was one other major difference from the pop side. The first generation of rappers didn't have real management or attorneys to review contracts. They didn't have a Russell Simmons in their corner. So while Rodgers and Edwards immediately got their cut, Caz remains uncredited and unpaid for his work. Never mind that Jackson dropped Brown's DJ name, Casanova Fly, during his verse.

Brown had handed over his lyrics to a pizza guy. That pizza guy kept that convenient fact to himself as he rode the quirky hit to become the accidental star Big Bank Hank.

"I didn't know at the time, of course, when everybody heard the Sugarhill Gang. We thought this is the greatest rap ever," said Ice-T, a longtime Caz admirer. "But then, after I met Caz, the word kind of got out that Caz wrote that rhyme. 'I'm the C-A-S-AN, the O-V-A, and the rest is F-L-Y.' When you're going to steal somebody's rap, you don't steal somebody's name, too. It's blatant it was done like that."

• • •

"Rapper's Delight" not only made stars of Big Bank Hank, Wonder Mike, and Master Gee—who were saluted by Don Cornelius on *Soul Train* and toured the world—it also turned Sugar Hill Records into a major player, flush with cash and ready to expand. They signed up Grandmaster Flash and the Furious Five, the Treacherous Three, and the Funky 4+1. All of those groups—legit, not manufactured—would ultimately regret their deals. Many ended up broke and stuck in legal limbo.

Sonically, the Sugar Hill artists were also stuck. The Robinsons' musical meat grinder turned hard beats into marmalade, all of the R&B designed to return Sugar Hill to the Top 40. That may have bothered the authentic B-boys. Robert "Rocky" Ford, though, couldn't have cared less.

"The only thing that bothered me about 'Rapper's Delight,'" said Ford, "is it came out first."

To Ford, "Rapper's Delight" offered a completely new model. You could take some version of what you heard in the clubs, put it on vinyl, and actually make money. The single had hit number thirty-six in the United States, peaked at three in the UK, and sold more than a million copies, though Sugar Hill's murky business practices made it hard to know exactly how many.

Within weeks, Ford and J. B. Moore, a coworker in the advertising department at *Billboard*, were plotting out their musical response to the Robinsons. That's when Ford tracked down his old bass-playing buddy. He needed somebody who knew music. And Larry Smith, up in Toronto for *Indigo*, headed back to New York.

Smith kept "Rapper's Delight" in mind as he hit the studio.

"We wanted a record to compete with that," Smith would say later. "We were trying for something that didn't copy it, but *felt* like it. And that's what we came up with, after woodshedding for a while."

Moore wrote the lyrics for what became "Christmas Rappin'." They were not meant ("gonna shake it, gonna bake it, gonna make it good") to win the Booker Prize. His and Ford's first choice to rap them was Eddie Cheba, but Russell Simmons had his own idea. He took Ford to see his guy Kurtis Blow at the Hotel Diplomat. That did the trick.

"Kurtis had the looks. And Kurtis, to me, was the nicest-looking kid I got to meet, and he didn't have the big ego like a lot of the rappers did at the time," said Ford. "And he was very approachable, because he didn't write, himself, at that point. J. B. and I, being writers, we needed to have somebody we could write songs for. Kurtis didn't have any ideas. Which for us was a boon."

Kurtis Walker, the original King of Rap, came from Harlem and had been kicked out of high school for dealing drugs. Walker was bright; smart enough to get his GED and enroll at the City College of New York to study communications. The drugs were strictly small time, something to keep his wallet warm. Kurt's true love was music. He became a regular at the clubs and learned how to work the turntables. By 1976, he performed as Kool DJ Kurt. He became Kurtis Blow after that.

He did have the looks. Those sideburns, the easy smile, and a tightly cropped Afro. He could dance, and he looked cool even in his disco uniform, with the fat lapels and buttoned-up vest. It's easy to understand why he jumped out from behind the turntable and onto the front of the stage.

Then there was his manager. Simmons, the middle brother in the house, joined a local gang, the Seven Crowns, but it was clear he was no killer.

"I had heard stories, but I had never seen that in him," said Walker. "I didn't believe it. Hollis, Queens, is a pretty tough neighborhood. And you've got to be something to survive in that neighborhood. But my whole thing was, I was from Harlem, and so I was around real killers who were real gangsters. Real murderers. These guys used to rob stores. My crew from my neighborhood, eighty percent of them are dead, my brother included."

The first thing Kurt noticed was Russell's dancing. He could do the Hustle. He also couldn't shut up. He made an impression, and that's why, when Kurt spotted Russ one day at City College, he shouted out, "I know you."

They became friends, clubbing together, promoting parties, and trying to get DJs to play the disco singles Simmons was pushing.

"We would go to all the gay clubs that nobody could get in," said Simmons. "And we could get in. Me, Kurtis Blow, all the Harlem cats. If you go down there long enough, you make enough friends. I was a member eventually at Paradise Garage. And the Loft, they just let me in the Loft. We would go in there and smoke dust and be high as fuck and there would be a lot of lesbian girls. It was cool. We would go all the time. And then eventually, when I had to promote records, I would go on the Track."

There was Bentley's, where everybody wore suits and Russell slid through with sneakers. There was Club 371, where Reggie Wells served as music director and DJ Hollywood and Lovebug and Cheba took the mic. These days, you'll hear grumbling about the raps, that they were cheesy disco and R&B, but those spots were the bridge between a normal supper club and what became the main stage for them all, Disco Fever.

Albert Abbatiello opened it in 1976 as a neighborhood bar in the South Bronx. It struggled, so he let his son, Sal, take it over. Sal turned it into a dance club. He renamed it Disco Fever in response to *Saturday Night Fever*, the smash movie starring John Travolta.

And he started with Grandmaster Flash on a Tuesday night in 1977, charging one dollar at the door. Soon, it was Tuesday night every night. By the early '80s, the Fever would be recognized as "the rap capitol of the Solar System," the words then journalist Bill Adler used in a 1983 profile of Russell Simmons for *People* magazine.

The Fever was a gathering spot, the center of the party, but also an easily accessible focus group. When Sylvia Robinson had a song she thought would be bigger than "Rapper's Delight," she called Abbatiello. That's where Abbatiello heard Melle Mel's rhymes on "The Message," arguably hip-hop's first socially conscious hit, for the first time. On the floor.

"The minute they made a record, they would come to the Fever and test it," said Abbatiello. "As they were producing it. They would see what's missing. That alive fucking testing group."

That's where Simmons would see the first generation of MCs and DJs, from Spoonie Gee to Flash to the Cold Crush. But it was DJ Hollywood he considered the "greatest rapper who ever lived."

"And they'd argue, he wasn't hip-hop," said Simmons. "He would sell five thousand tickets. 'What did y'all sell. Y'all played the park.' There wouldn't be a rap record without DJ Hollywood. He may not have said it first. But he said in a way the speakers would vibrate, and he'd put the mic down and nobody would touch the mic."

• • •

The Fever was important. But ultimately, a club is just a room with walls and a ceiling. The energy, the dynamic, the drama that sparked the birth of hip-hop couldn't be contained under a single roof. It was about more of a moment and a philosophy, of a series of touchpoints in art, dance, and sound reaching a captive audience. What the movement had in common with others—the Harlem Renaissance of the 1920s, the Summer of Love explosion in San Francisco's Haight—is that it crossed geographical, economic, and, most important, racial lines. In New York, it linked the uptown (black) with the downtown (white), which was no small thing, particularly in a city defined by a catchphrase, "The Bronx Is Burning." They said that television sportscaster Howard Cosell used that line, but he actually never did. Cosell was on the air during Game 2 of the 1977 World Series when the surreal images of a raging fire, outside Yankee Stadium, were broadcast on ABC, images he did describe.

The flames inspired a book and, eventually, a miniseries based on that book. It also drew former California governor Ronald Reagan to the Bronx for a tense visit when he was running for president and wanted to highlight the country's economic problems during Jimmy Carter's tenure.

"This is a disgrace and should not be allowed to go on," he said after losing his temper out of frustration as people shouted complaints to him.

The seemingly endless swaths of abandoned, burned-out buildings and garbage-strewn, empty lots defined so much of the aesthetic of the work of street photographer Joe Conzo and Ahearn's *Wild Style*.

But the Bronx was also home base for Kool Herc, who, in that community room on Sedgwick Avenue, worked the turntables the night hip-hop was supposedly born. The Bronx would also spawn so many pioneers, including the Cold Crush, Grandmaster Flash, Melle Mel, and, later, Slick Rick and Boogie Down Productions.

Hip-hop really did start in the streets. You didn't have to be eighteen to get into a park jam, for one thing. The clubs then turned the music into something else, something that could be commodified and monetized. The clubs were also a place where figurative walls of race, geography, and social strata could be knocked down.

In those days, you could walk into an all-black club and see Rick Rubin, the college kid from Long Island, at the DJ booth shooting the shit with Jazzy Jay. You might see Ahearn snapping photos of Lovebug setting up the decks as Busy Bee and Caz hovered over.

Glenn O'Brien, the Georgetown-educated scenester, helped make one of the most important introductions in those days, an intro that created an immediate, multicultural bridge. He did it through the platform he created as host of a New York cable access program called *TV Party*, a free-form variety show that ran from 1978 to 1982.

"Cable TV was in its infancy," said Chris Stein, Blondie's guitarist and a friend of O'Brien. "There was some law in place that they had to devote a couple of stations to public access. A forum for anybody who wanted to put anything on. There was a lady named Coco Crystal. She's an old New Yorker. She did a TV show named *If I Can't Dance, You Can Keep Your Revolution*. She would just sit around and interview people and everyone would smoke pot on it. Glenn was on the show one night and the next day he was on the subway and a couple of people came up to him and said, 'Oh, we saw you on TV last night.' The lightbulb went off in his head and so we started doing this live TV broadcast. It was under a hundred dollars to put on a show.

Everybody would meet at the TV studio and we'd do this hour show."

TV Party blended comedy and music and was so deliciously unpredictable that David Letterman, the host of NBC's new late-night talk show, listed it as a favorite in a newspaper survey taken in the early '80s. The late O'Brien once described the show as "seizing television and using it for democratic purposes." He mentioned Hugh Hefner's short-lived *Playboy After Dark* as an inspiration. But *TV Party* really wasn't at all like Hef's stiff and staged gatherings, where the tuxedoed magazine founder forced his miniskirted minions to clap along to Three Dog Night as cameras darted around his swinging pad. *TV Party* felt looser and less important and certainly less contrived.

O'Brien, trim, handsome, and often in shades, served as host, with Stein as his sidekick. Fred Brathwaite, who had started out by hosting a radio show when he attended Medgar Evers College in Brooklyn, worked the cameras and also the microphones.

Brathwaite, soon to be known as Fab 5 Freddy, had been drawn to O'Brien through the punk rock column he wrote for *Interview* magazine starting in 1979.

Actually, "Glenn O'Brien's Beat" didn't just cover punk rock. O'Brien wrote about punk, new wave, disco, and the beginning of dancehall reggae. "Which I was hearing," said Brathwaite, "but Glenn wrote so authoritatively and so informatively. I was learning more from this column. I was just a big fan and I reached out and he was receptive and embracing and kind of became a mentor to me."

Another mentor was stepping up. O'Brien was twelve years

older than Freddy. He had deep connections to New York culture having worked for Andy Warhol at *Interview*. He would live a fascinating, rich life, with a résumé that would leap from editing Madonna's *Sex* book to serving as creative director for Barneys New York and helping found *Spin* magazine. But in terms of culture-mashing, O'Brien's greatest contribution may have been *TV Party*.

"This is not a test," O'Brien shouted during one opening over a free-form jam. "This is an actual show."

TV Party's guest list included the New York hipsters he already knew, including Blondie's Debbie Harry and the Talking Heads' singer David Byrne. But he also brought in anyone he appreciated who might be open to hanging out. That included George Clinton, David Bowie, and the Clash's Mick Jones, as well as artists Chris Burden, Jean-Michel Basquiat, and Robert Mapplethorpe. *TV Party* could devolve into just about anything. Comedy skits. An hour of sludgy, improvised guitar metal. Harry on a pogo stick.

For Brathwaite, the show's strength was bringing together a city that was intensely polarized, cut along racial and class lines. In that studio, barriers dissolved.

"We were all just looked at as weirdoes and freaks by most normal people," said Brathwaite. "Just filmmakers, painters, writers, photographers. A small group, but definitely the kind of epicenter of the zeitgeist of downtown culture at the time."

It was Brathwaite who helped O'Brien orchestrate one of the first, important rock-rap collaborations. One night, he organized an outing with Stein and Harry to a community center in the Bronx to check out a hip-hop party.

"Debbie, me, and Glenn were definitely the only white people there," remembered Stein. "It was great. The energy was fantastic. It was the Funky 4+1, maybe the Cold Crush, and Flash was definitely there. I remember totally appreciating this was going on uptown while we were doing our thing downtown."

The experience inspired "Rapture," a song that would be released twelve days into 1981 as the second single off Blondie's *Autoamerican* album. "Rapture" is sometimes pitched as the first true rock-rap collaboration. That depends on your definition. There is a section during which Harry raps and name checks Grandmaster Flash, but her rhyming—and her rhymes—weren't about to give Melle Mel a run for his gold chains.

What Blondie's "Rapture" did, though, was share a glimpse of the downtown universe with a wider audience. The video for the song, which went to number one, featured Basquiat at a turntable, and Brathwaite and artist Lee Quinones with spray cans working on a color-blasting wall of graffiti. (The scene, oddly enough, also included a child ballerina and a woman walking a goat down the street.)

And when Blondie hosted *Saturday Night Live* the next year, they brought out the Funky 4+1 to perform "That's the Joint"—the first appearance on national television for a rap group. But that melding of different crowds had already been underway off camera. If Harry and Stein could go uptown to hang with Flash or Freddy, the Funky 4+1 could come downtown, into Manhattan, and play what were once white clubs.

"There was a point where hip-hop and punk were being integrated," said Sha-Rock, the 1 in the Funky 4. "We was playing a place like the Ritz in Manhattan. The Mudd Club. All these clubs in the Village where you had punk rockers. The crowd, they'd be throwing each other up in the air and it was strange, but that let us know they were feeling us."

"That's the story of popular culture in America," said Brathwaite. "It's been a collaborative effort between blacks, Jews, and Italians, particularly in New York. That's how everything kind of happened in this place."

Russell Simmons was watching this. He saw Brathwaite in Ahearn's feature-length film *Wild Style*, which starred Quinones and featured a soundtrack crafted by Grandmaster Caz and Stein. Simmons understood the connection between Blondie and the uptown rappers. In 1982, when Simmons set up his Rush Management office at 1133 Broadway in Manhattan, he and Brathwaite were among the few black people in the mix downtown. But they were there. And it wasn't a coincidence that when it came time for Simmons to build his empire, he didn't just include his Hollis buddies. He signed on Adler and eventually brought in Rubin and Cohen. Were they going to be best friends? No. But there was one thing the trio had in common. They were outsiders who didn't believe in limits.

Chapter 4

AEROSMITH: WHO GOT THE BEAT?

Nobody argues with how the riff came about. That was all Joe Perry.

"I was really into the Meters, the esoteric, funky kind of music," he said. "Sly and the Family Stone. I started fooling around on this riff."

The next part is where things get murky. It's one thing to argue over a songwriting credit, but a drumbeat?

Ask Steven Tyler and he doesn't hesitate. It is December 15, 1974. The band is in Hawaii, opening for the Guess Who at the Honolulu International Center. During sound check, Perry is onstage, chugging through the riff. Tyler, originally a drummer but now two records into his reign as lead singer, hops behind Joey Kramer's kit.

"I ran out from the dressing room and started playing," Tyler said. "I came up with it. Let's just leave it at that. I'm a drummer at heart."

It's a nice story and one that he repeated over the years. But the drummer, the actual Aerosmith drummer, said it's not true.

"Steven," Joey Kramer said, "is full of shit."

Bear in mind, this discussion didn't take place years after a breakup or a litany of lawsuits. It wasn't about money. You don't get royalties for a beat. This beef was about something deeper and more complex, a blend of pride and also power, a DNA strand of the emotional psychodrama that twists through any family, whether one linked by blood or a recording contract.

Strangely enough, it was a disagreement between two members of an active band that, in 2019, is still touring, talking, and plotting out a new record. Kramer moves the action approximately 5,062 miles to the east.

"Not only was it not in Hawaii," continued Kramer, "but it was at a studio in Framingham, Massachusetts. I don't know if it was before Hawaii or after Hawaii. I remember Joe playing the riff and me playing what I played to the riff. I don't remember Steven having anything to do with it."

It's no easier to dig deeper for the origin story of one of the great beats in rock—and one of the most influential breakbeats in hip-hop history.

Jack Douglas, the group's mentoring producer during its 1970s golden era, offered his view. He was on team Tyler, though with some misgivings.

"Steven came up with it," said Douglas, who produced "Walk This Way." "He's a drummer and Joey embellished on it with the high-hat figure. But the basic part. Steven would come into a production with drum figures that he wanted to do something with. And that was one of them."

So it was Tyler? Here, Douglas, a spectacular storyteller with a flair for detail, took a step back from the story to make a request. Maybe, he said, this was a subject best left undiscussed.

"It has cost Joey much pain and a couple of mental breakdowns," he said. "Perhaps it's best to make it one of the great mysteries of life and let the reader weigh the evidence."

Well.

"Did Steven or Joey invent it?" said guitarist Brad Whitford. "I think the jury's still out on that. Now, Steven is a drummer at heart and a very inventive, creative drummer. So I don't know. I wasn't there when Joe and Steven were banging that around, and we messed with that song a lot. And then you have to take into consideration that Steven would probably take credit for everything that's on every Aerosmith record."

Perry had multiple takes. The first time he was asked, early in 2016, he left the answer somewhere in the middle.

"I asked Joey to play basic, straight twos and fours," said Perry. "Like an AC/DC song. If I had a drum machine, I would have done it. And Steven heard it, and I think he came up onstage and sat down at the drums and played something a little bit different than Joey was doing."

He paused. "I'm not sure."

Almost a year later, after hearing about the debate and Douglas's take, Perry leaned toward Tyler.

"They both had a hand in that, but the main 'bom da, be dom da da.' That one part is something that, after talking to Jack, Steven played that part," said Perry. "As far as the rest of it, the swing and the feel and all that, that's Joey. I think it's probably both of them."

Whitford didn't laugh when he was told of each account.

"Gosh, look how old we are and I don't know why we aren't able to rest a little bit with some of this stuff," he said. "A lot of this stuff is very important to Steven, but I couldn't tell you why. I mean, he just can be brutal and really very tough on Joey and his drumming."

• • •

The beat was a debate with a larger meaning, a debate that shed light on the complicated dynamic between Tyler and Kramer. That relationship was far better understood later, as therapy replaced self-medication, and as the gap of time between tours and recordings grew enough to allow these men time and space to develop perspective.

Not that there was peace. There is a reason in recent years Tyler had his own manager and Perry and the others had their own. There was a fundamental lack of trust within Aerosmith, though not enough to derail their status as one of classic rock's few survivors.

For Kramer, so much was defined by his difficult childhood and the connection he made between Mickey, his abusive father, and Tyler, his abusive lead singer. First Mickey. He was an advertising man who had served in World War II, been badly wounded, and remained haunted by what he saw on the battlefield. He and his wife, Doris, had four children—Joey and his three younger sisters. Mickey wouldn't touch the girls, but Joey was beaten regularly. He spent much of childhood seeking refuge in a crawl space, a place he felt safe. Doris not only failed to help him with Mickey. She once smashed a mirror over her son's head in anger.

Then Kramer joined Aerosmith, a band led by an overwhelming, overpowering front man who also happened to play the same instrument. And Steven Tyler wasn't satisfied holding a tambourine. He loved to play the drums. He was also quite good. That means he wasn't about to leave Kramer alone. He would push him to play the rhythms that were in his head. Or, on the flip side, yell at him when he didn't play the rhythms in his head. Post-gig rides to the hotel or airport brought blistering attacks.

"He could be brutal," said Whitford. "Just berating him."

"I would sit in the back of a car and listen to him telling me how much I fucking sucked and why don't I get my fucking shit together," Kramer said. "Why am I doing this and why would I do that and why, why, why, why? And I don't think anybody would have taken what he was giving me and dealt with it the same way that I dealt with it."

Later, in therapy, after an emotional breakdown and briefly leaving Aerosmith, Kramer made the obvious connection between Tyler and Mickey and his lifelong confusion between love and abuse. Because Tyler could be so loving. He could lean in, put his arm around you, and suddenly you were the only one in the room. Until you're a piece of shit.

"You know you're attracted to people who abuse you and you mistake that for love," said Kramer. "Thus, the confusion between love and abuse. And that was my main downfall. He had me convinced that he loved me. So I was listening to him."

Tyler, naturally, had a different view. We had spoken twice before I talked to Kramer, so the subject hadn't come up. Later, after talking to Joey, I tried to get Steven back on the phone. He said he was thick into rehearsals for the band's upcoming tour and first brushed me off. I pressed harder and wrote him a text telling him that Kramer had called the singer "emotionally abusive."

I thought that might spark a phone call. Instead, Tyler responded with a simple, unforgiving text.

"James Brown's band . . . Buddy Rich . . . the Who . . . they all went through lots of crazy internal yelling to get it right . . . I felt the need to do whatever it took to get it right . . . And somehow down the line . . . I have to believe I did."

• • •

Back to the beat.

About a year after Tyler first told me his account, I brought the subject up with him again. I thought a second interrogation might expose any inconsistencies in his account. But when Tyler spoke, he sounded as sure of himself as ever.

"I remember like it was twenty minutes ago. We were on tour. We'd never played in Hawaii. It was the first tour in Hawaii. Joe and I were really excited, because after we played Honolulu in a place called HIC auditorium we got a chance to get on a plane with our significant others and go to Maui. We always wanted to go to Maui. It was always like Hawaiian and tropical and let's go scuba diving. So Joe and I went. But I digress. I was in the dressing room with the whole band and Joe went out, he was onstage and he was checking his amps to make sure they played on twelve. And he starts playing this riff and I freaked. And we were all waiting for a connection. As I ran out, as I quite often do, if Joey's not sitting on the drums, well, fuck me. I'm out there and I always jam with Joe. In fact, that's how we wrote songs. At the time he was going through this [Tyler sings the "Walk This Way" riff] and doing that groovy rhythm that, if we were a three piece, would work fine. And I went, 'What the fuck are you doing, man? How are you doing that? Are you doing it with your fingers or with a pick?' But I sat behind the drums, and the rest is history."

I asked about the possibility that they both invented that beat, if Kramer at least created the high-hat snap.

"Oh god, he might have," Tyler said. "I don't know if we're nitpicking here. I just remember sitting down and doing that, and I'm really proud of it. Amen."

Now Kramer's second spin.

"Steven can say and do whatever it is that he chooses," he countered. "That's what he believes to be the truth. I'm not going to change his mind. I know the truth in my heart, and the people that were there that witnessed it know the truth in their hearts. And you know that's as far as it goes. I'm not interested in making, you know, a mountain out of a molehill. At the same time, that beat, which is my beat, is probably the most copied and most used rock and roll beat ever in history. You know how many rap records and hip-hop records have that beat on it? And believe me, I'm not that kind of guy. I'm not looking for credit."

Except that credit, in this case, speaks to a larger, more pervasive issue within the band. It is not just linked to his father, the abuse, the recovery, the understanding of vulnerabilities and how to protect yourself from them. Credit is tied into the entire culture of Aerosmith and any rock band. The singer and lead guitarist stand out front. The rhythm section may be vital to the sound, but it's also always replaceable. Who plays bass for the Rolling Stones? Exactly. In Aerosmith's case, you were always reminded. There was Tyler and Perry at the front and everybody else down in steerage.

That's when Kramer was asked about the unflattering term John Kalodner, the famed record executive who would eventually sign Aerosmith, used to describe Kramer, Whitford, and Hamilton: the less important three.

All of that, Kramer said, was why he was still talking about who invented a beat back when Gerald Ford was president.

"Because it's never enough, man, for the same reason that Brad and I and Tom were the LI3," said Kramer. "Because it's never enough. Steven wants it all for himself."

• • •

At least everybody could agree on who wrote the lyrics. The words are a key element to the rhythmic thrust of "Walk This Way." Content-wise, "Walk" isn't really about anything, unless you're trying to set a land-speed record for creepy sexual references per verse. The context does matter. Tyler, when he wrote the song, was locked in a relationship with Julia Holcomb. She was sixteen when they met in late 1973, and they would stay together for three years.

In the song, there's the cheerleader who's a "real young bleeder," her sister and her cousin, a "missy" at the high school dance, three young ladies in the locker room, the next-door neighbor's daughter, and a schoolgirl sweetie with her "skirt's climbing way up her knee."

Okay. So what makes "Walk This Way" magical isn't the meaning. It's the delivery, delivered shotgun style, peppered with apostrophes to replace almost every hard *g*.

See-saw swingin' with the boys in the school
With your feet flyin' up in the air

Singin' hey diddle-diddle with the kitty in the middle
You be swingin' like you just didn't care

"If you listen to the cadence, the way Steven sings, it's almost a rap," said Richie Sambora, the former Bon Jovi guitarist. "He just puts a melody on top of it. 'Walk This Way' was the predecessor of white rap in a way."

The words came in early 1975 as the band gathered at the Record Plant in New York City to work on their third album, *Toys in the Attic*. Some bands would spend months in preproduction, tightening up the songs they'd jammed through on the road and arrive at the studio ready to record. During Aerosmith's glorious rise, that only happened once, on *Get Your Wings*.

"After that, they never had any material," said Douglas. "No lyrics. Just germs. 'One of you guys have a song? Yeah, I have this. *De do der.* Anybody want to add anything to that? *Do de dee dip.* All right. Maybe you should change that key and slow it down so we can put these two together.' That's how it was. They came in with licks and we sat collectively and put the licks together like sewing together a quilt to get something, to build a track. Then after the track was built, the very last thing that happened, which was the lyrics. And they took forever and it was like pulling teeth to get them, but they came."

In the case of *Toys*, the album was basically finished, but they had this irresistible, wordless backing track left over. On a Sunday afternoon, Douglas and the band decided to take a long walk down Eighth Avenue to Times Square. This was 1975, long before the city scrubbed down the area, installing pedestrian plazas and latte shacks. This was the Times Square of Scorsese's *Taxi Driver*, pimps and drug dealers and triple-X movie houses. That's where they saw the light—or, more specifically, a Mel Brooks classic.

"The whole band was there that day because we really wanted to get it down," remembered Douglas. "Being Sunday afternoon, there was absolutely no one on the street. When we got to Forty-second Street, *Young Frankenstein* was playing. The whole band went in, and when that line came up—'Walk this way'—we were in hysterics, and when we got back to the studio, I started walking around like Marty Feldman. A bit of a joke. And Steven said, 'Wait a minute.' So the chorus came first, and about two hours later the verse came."

At first, "Walk This Way" wouldn't even be the biggest hit on *Toys in the Attic*. That would be "Sweet Emotion," with its wall of guitar and Tyler's spitting takedown of Perry's belle. "Walk" didn't even chart when it was first released as a single at the end of August 1975. But the song did catch on a year later when Aerosmith reissued it, peaking at number ten on January 29, 1977. Historically, there's no denying its significance.

"Walk" was the first Aerosmith song Saul Hudson, a ten-year-old Jewish kid in Los Angeles, would hear. A little over a decade later, he would be known as Slash, and his band, Guns N' Roses, would be opening for Aerosmith.

"It was and still is one of the most exciting lyrics about teenage sexuality I've ever heard, and one of the best fucking guitar riffs of all time," he said.

• • •

The song's reach was undeniable, a reach that extended well beyond the white kids listening to rock radio. What made "Walk" special, transcendent, is how far it traveled. DJs scouring record bins in New York City connected with *Toys in the Attic*. They weren't interested in how Tyler tied those scarves to his microphone, or the legend of the Toxic Twins, or the possibilities of scoring a ticket to the next gig at the Garden. The DJs weren't even particularly interested in what Aerosmith called the song. But as early as 1977, they were rapping to the song's beat.

"We had a routine with 'Walk This Way,' but we would call it Aerosmith," said the Funky 4+1's Sha-Rock.

In New York City, a kid from Barbados named Joseph Saddler went through his record store routine. He sliced open the plastic wrap on a copy of *Toys in the Attic* and removed the LP from the sleeve. Song four looked promising to the young DJ.

"I was able to take one copy out and look at the vinyl in the light and see that it was pretty shallow," he said. "And when it's shallow that means it is mild accompaniment in the song. That *Toys in the Attic*, when I got that, it was relatively new."

Other DJs also discovered Aerosmith this way. Everything began with that groove. They were unbiased when it came to finding the beat.

"The beat could have been from Stravinsky," said Public Enemy's Chuck D. "Out of that psychology comes this idea that music is music. That was an oversight by the critics and the journalists and an awful lot of the people who were trying to make judgment calls on what rap was and wasn't. They would try to say it was an urban culture. They just knew the DJ was doing something and the rapper was on top of it and the dancers were on top of it. A lot of them didn't delve into the alchemy of what was used by the DJ."

By the time he found "Walk This Way," Saddler was going by Grandmaster Flash. He spent endless hours in his bedroom until he could loop, scratch, and punch into a record in ways that would revolutionize music. He also formed a group with Melle Mel (Melvin Glover), Cowboy (Keith Wiggins), Kidd Creole (Nathaniel Glover), Rahiem (Guy Todd Williams), and Scorpio (Eddie Morris). It is Scorpio you'll hear on a 1978 tape—eight years before Run-DMC released *Raising Hell*—loaded up onto YouTube.

"Flash was called Flash for a reason," said Chuck D. "Flash was called Flash because he could extend it with speed to not even have you hear the guitars. That record was done for hip-hop after forty-five seconds."

So on that ancient tape, you don't hear Tyler's voice. On the street, "Walk This Way" was about the beat, and the turntablism that allowed you to extend it. It certainly wasn't about the singer.

Chapter 5

RUN-DMC: IT'S LIKE THAT

There would always, of course, be a genetic imbalance when it came to Run-DMC. Calling it nepotism doesn't begin to describe it. And that reality—of Run's older brother being the manager—would eventually create a poisonous dynamic, whether they would admit it or not.

But you could argue that that's looking at the smaller picture. It is because of Russell Simmons that they ever had anything to fight about. Simmons wasn't just a guy booking dates. He had that rare gift, that vision that would make him one of the most successful black entertainment entrepreneurs of the twentieth century. He would start with music, then move into fashion and comedy and even yoga studios. He would eventually be worth more than $300 million. (That legacy would be tarnished in 2017 after a group of women accused Simmons of sexually assaulting them over a period stretching from the 1980s until recently. Simmons denied the accusations and no charges were filed. But the damage was done. He would resign from his companies, he said, to focus on his "personal growth, spiritual learning, and above all listening.")

As rap moved from the playgrounds into the recording studio, Rush clients would benefit from having Simmons in their corner.

"The thing that separated Grandmaster Flash from

Run-DMC was management," said Cey Adams, the graffiti kid who became one of the most influential artists in hip-hop as Def Jam's creative director. "That was the difference between any of those other bands and the bands managed by Rush. That's why they were on national tours. That's why they got endorsement deals."

The brotherly bond, though, did bring Run the kind of security DMC and Jay never could have.

It meant he would never have to live in fear. Even if he went bankrupt, even if he wasn't always able to collect his royalties—both of which occurred—he could be found living in a New Jersey mansion with a swimming pool and a basketball court. Jay, by the end of his too-short life, was in massive debt.

D also found life a struggle. After *Raising Hell*'s unprecedented success, he wanted more of a creative voice and, as Run and Jay ignored those wants, he began to grow resentful. His proudly public, performance-like consumption of Olde English became a private drinking problem. The revelation that he was adopted sent a jarring jolt through the Son of Byford. Then, the unthinkable. DMC lost his voice. Is there any greater indignity for an MC?

• • •

There is a reason to consider the end before we dig into the start. Because understanding where Run and DMC ended up is important in understanding the different way they each see the past. Many of the details are the same. The interpretation is not.

To Run, it was a glorious time, when two friends came together to develop the team that would take on all comers. They became masters in D's basement, took that to the wider world, and developed an unbeatable partnership. It wasn't always easy. He fought to get D in the group in the beginning, when Russell wanted Joey to launch a solo career. That, Run said, was proof of his undying loyalty.

D had a cooler take. He said that he had nothing against Run. He didn't hate him. But he also was not sentimental about their relationship.

"Run," he said, "fought to get me in the group for two reasons. He didn't want to be alone, because he's not that person that could be alone. And he knew this motherfucker Darryl has got some shit in them books. People thought we came together because of love. I said, no, hip-hop brought me and Run together. And the business of hip-hop is what tore us apart."

File that conflict away for a moment and step back in time. Because whatever they felt later on, there was a moment when everything was funky fresh and none of that bitterness, tension, or record biz reality had entered the scene.

Run reiterated that he wasn't Russell's puppet. What better example than how he got his friend in the group.

"Russell's idea was to make a solo artist out of Run," said Bill Adler, the veteran journalist who would become the publicity head for Rush, Def Jam, and the de facto historian of the golden rap age. "It was Joe, on his own, who said, 'No, that's not how it's going to be.' And it was also Joe who reached out to Jason. Let's be clear that Joe pulled the group together. He was ebullient. He was a dynamo. He was just blazing. He was very high energy, very charming, very funny. And he was the leader of the group."

Creatively, Joe and Darryl were the perfect duo. Run was the fireball—part comic, part naughty schoolboy—always ready to take the spotlight. D was the quiet one with the earth-shattering rhyme book and the call of a stone-cold closer. Never power hungry, never looking for attention, barely speaking during interviews.

"People knew me through my lyrics," said DMC. "Everybody was like, Run was the attitude, Jay was the style, but what's up with that quiet motherfucker DMC with the glasses? You learned about my family through 'Son of Byford.' You learned what I liked to eat through 'Sucker M.C.'s.' I never spoke at business meetings or interviews. I didn't have to say nothing, because Run was the front man. I just knew I'm showing up and I'm fucking kicking Moe Dee's ass when I get the chance."

Run and D would not just be partners. They became the most important team in rap. And make no mistake about it. They were a team.

Consider the development of "It's Like That," the first important Run-DMC side and a song that predates Jam Master Jay's joining the group.

"It's Like That" started when Run called Darryl and told him he had an idea for a song.

He had been thinking about Kurtis Blow's "Tough," the lead and title track on Blow's third album, which was released in 1982.

Livin' on the uptown side of jive
Hustlin' a buck to stay alive
Lookin' for a ten and they give you five
Well, it's tough

"My brain said, 'Eh, okay, Kurtis wrote a record about life being tough,'" said Run. "I'm going to write a record about it just is."

The difference, he said, was his attitude. He wanted to create a more abstract, more philosophical take on life's struggles, nothing pessimistic.

"It is what it is. You've heard that. Well, your life falls apart like that. Not, it's tough. No complaining was my thing, I guess."

He went to DMC, who drew on his own inspiration—Melle Mel and Duke Bootee's "Message II (Survival)."

"So he takes everything like Grandmaster Caz and he flips it," said Run. "He's like, it's not 'It's Like That.' It's 'It's Like That and That's the Way It Is.'"

Telling the story, Run paused again for dramatic effect.

"Oh my god," he said. "Now 'It's Like That' has a double hook."

From there, they went to Larry Smith's attic to lay down a demo. That was when DMC spoke up.

He took issue with Run's delivery. Too corny, too Kurtis Blow. He explained by rapping it out, and also with his very strong response to a demo that Smith had recorded.

"When Larry put that on, I'll never forget. I had a quart of Olde English. Forty-ouncers wasn't out yet. And when I heard that, I was like, 'Yo, this is bullshit. Did you hear *Planet fucking Rock*? Did you hear what the fucking Zulu Nation is doing?'"

The Soul Sonic Force—Mr. Biggs, Pow Wow, and
M.C. Globe
We emphasize to show, we got ego

It wasn't like Run and Larry were trying to do cheesy disco. They were listening.

"Larry and Joe, they was like, 'Yo, that's real dope,'" said DMC. "Joe was busy trying to be Kurtis Blow, what Russell was already doing. I was busy trying to pretend to bust Melle Mel and Kurtis Blow's ass. I had no idea it was going to come true."

• • •

They had the single. Now they had to find somebody to put it out.

As he looked for a label, Russell Simmons found it only natural to stop by the Fifty-seventh Street offices of Profile Records. He knew Cory Robbins from when he had worked with Kurtis Blow on "Christmas Rappin'."

That was the song Rocky Ford and J. B. Moore had signed Blow for. Robbins had sour memories of that experience. He had heard "Christmas Rappin'," wanted to take a shot at it, and offered the producing team a much-needed $10,000 for an advance to hurry into the studio to record it. With Christmas approaching, there wasn't time to get the lawyers to dot the *i*'s and cross the *t*'s on a contract—usually how Robbins did business. And he would pay for that.

Right before they began pressing "Christmas Rappin'," Ford and Moore called Robbins to tell him Mercury Records wanted to sign Blow. That would make Blow's single the first rap song on a major label.

"I was heartbroken," said Robbins. "I don't think I've talked to either of those guys to this day, because they totally went against their word and made me look bad."

There was no beef with Simmons, though. Robbins also had an added layer of protection, a hard-driving partner who made it his business not to be taken advantage of.

Steve Plotnicki and Cory Robbins were both music-obsessed Jewish kids who never got through college. Robbins, from Nyack, a suburb thirty-five miles north of New York City, developed a deep connection to rock and roll as a boy. His grandfather, who owned a bar, would give him the worn 45s from the jukebox when he was updating the Seeburg with new vinyl.

Robbins studied the pop charts and picked up a Gibson SG Standard before his bar mitzvah. In high school, he got a summer job at Midland Records and dropped out of SUNY New Paltz after a year to work for MCA's publishing arm. His job was to search for songs that could be hits. That's when Blow briefly entered and exited his life. Robbins then started his own label.

He connected with Plotnicki without having any idea that they would eventually become partners.

Plotnicki had cowritten a disco song called "Love Insurance." Lou Levy, Robbins's boss at MCA Music Publishing, handed him the tape.

"I heard it, I'm like, 'This is a really good song.' I called up the phone number on the cassette and Steve's mother answered the phone. I said, 'This is Cory Robbins from MCA Music Publishing,' and his mother, I guess, she kind of had a heart attack."

"Love Insurance," sung by Sharon Redd and credited to the Front Page, became a disco hit, and Plotnicki called Robbins almost every day to check in.

"I really liked his calls. He's fun. He's smart. We just got friendly," said Robbins. "I told him, 'Since you can write songs and I can produce records, maybe we can start our own label. We'll do this ourselves and keep all the money.'"

Plotnicki was the son of Holocaust survivors. This was an important, defining characteristic as the years went by, as his slate of conflicts and his roster of enemies grew. It is worth noting that though he developed a reputation as a serial litigator, Plotnicki rarely, if ever, started the fight. But if you picked one, if you dared to try to take what was rightfully his, he would not back down. He would also win.

This is how Plotnicki described his parents.

"They are vigilant about what they own, but they take offense to anybody that wants to limit them in anyway," he said. "They lived through an experience of losing everything—family, goods—and anything that approaches, they cut it off" is how he describes the survivor mentality.

Plotnicki grew up in Bayside, Queens. His father, born in Poland, was a kosher butcher. Plotnicki played guitar, loved the Grateful Dead, and felt swept up in the counterculture as a teenager during the Woodstock era. He tried six weeks at community college before realizing he didn't want to go to school.

He was twenty-five when "Love Insurance" became a hit. What struck him most wasn't the excitement of hearing his song on the radio. It was how little money he made. He recognized that there was another side, the business side.

"I made all of three thousand dollars," he said. "I thought, 'This is a shitty way to make a living.'"

Plotnicki became a salesman at a record wholesaler. It was 1980. Making his rounds, he noticed that there were only two things that sold well: disco and rap 12-inchers.

"I said, 'You know, there's a business here that we can start to make these disco and rap records,'" he remembered. "I really liked rap music back then. It was a combination of vulnerability, some class resentment, but they aspired to the things that my children would have had."

Robbins and Plotnicki each borrowed $17,000 from their parents and formed Profile in May 1981. They then promptly began to blow through their bank account. The label's first record was Grace Kennedy's "I'm Starting Again," a pop record with a disco beat that might sound like Blondie if you sucked out the energy and attitude. It stiffed. So did the second release, a reissue of Lonnie Love's "Young Ladies" rap. The third release was Gidea Park's Four Seasons medley "Seasons of Gold," which had already been a hit in England. It cracked the Top 100. That didn't solve the larger problem.

"We were on the edge of failure," said Plotnicki. "We were down to our last two thousand dollars. Until Dr. Jekyll and Mr. Hyde."

Lonnie Love, whose real name was Alonzo Brown, was Mr. Hyde. Andre Harrell, the future record company executive, became Dr. Jekyll. They followed the formula employed by Sugar Hill, rapping over somebody else's song—in this case "Genius of Love," a dance club smash for the Tom Tom Club that featured then Talking Heads members Tina Weymouth and Chris Frantz. The song became "Genius Rap."

Like "Rapper's Delight," "Genius Rap" didn't even pretend to be anything but a musical carbon copy of the original. Where Sugar Hill tried to get away with all-out theft, Profile credited the song to the Tom Tom Club from the start. The lyrics were the thing. They were a blend of flossing ("I got a penthouse on Central Park and I got a lovely view") and goofing ("We walk on water, fly through air, got a picture of myself in her underwear").

Robbins and Plotnicki made "Genius Rap" for $750. It sold more than 100,000 copies of the 12-inch single.

That's when Simmons came around.

He brought a tape to Robbins, curiously labeled *Runde-MC* in pen. The tape had the "It's Like That" demo recorded at Smith's house.

"That night, I go take a drive and I play that song over and over and over again," said Robbins. "By the end of the drive, I'm like, 'I think I should go sign this.'"

Plotnicki also heard the tape. He found it baffling.

"I hated it, really disliked it," he said. "But what do I understand about black kids from Hollis or the Bronx? You know what I mean? I don't understand anything about them."

What he and Robbins did have was their own mathematical formula for how to run an indie label. That formula meant they didn't have to fall in love with every song they put out. They just had to keep the costs down. This was Investment 101. A low-risk deal increased the payoff potential of a record hit.

"If I was running a venture capital fund, the way I would look at the world is, Well, I've got fifty million dollars," Plotnicki said. "That fifty million dollars, I'm going to invest in twenty-five businesses a year. And I expect four of them to hit, ten of them to break even, and the rest to go in the toilet. But the ones that hit, hit so big that that's where you make all the money. So when I said we need a record like this every month,

I was basically saying, Let's capitalize twelve records a year. It doesn't matter why we choose them. We're choosing them because they fit in the paradigm."

Robbins closed the deal with Russell Simmons. He gave him $2,000 to properly rerecord the "It's Like That" demo in a studio. And Smith and Simmons delivered a bonus. During the session, they had enough time to record a second track. Smith wanted to call it "Krush Groove." Robbins had another idea, taking his cue from one of the phrases Run used.

"Let's call it 'Sucker M.C.'s,'" he suggested.

• • •

They had a group, they had a single, they had a record label. Now they needed to get people to hear it. Manny Bella, Profile's radio promo guy, had worked in disco, pushing for radio play, but this was different. This was trying to sell something new to somebody who didn't want to buy it. The white radio stations were never going to be part of the conversation. The trouble is that the black radio stations also wouldn't give them a sniff.

"R&B hated us and we hated them," said Simmons. "We were from the hood. Black people that did R&B stuff wore alligator shoes and no socks. They were middle-class and didn't like the hood. Not only white America didn't want to hear from these niggas, it was black America, too. *Ebony* magazine put Run-DMC on the cover after *Rolling Stone.* BET played Run-DMC after MTV."

Bella remembered trying to break Run-DMC at WBLS. They were playing Peabo Bryson and Natalie Cole. The DJ Frankie

Crocker might even throw a Nat King Cole or Dinah Washington song into the mix. He certainly would not consider hip-hop.

So Bella came up with a time-honored strategy. He went to the competition. He went to Barry Mayo.

Mayo served as program director at WRKS-FM, Kiss 98.7. In the 1970s, the station had played Top 40, but in the summer of 1981, it shifted its format to what was called urban contemporary. Bella befriended Mayo and they started hanging out Friday nights, often at the Roxy. That's where the program director met Afrika Bambaataa, DJ Jazzy Jay, and Kool DJ Red Alert. Soon, he had recruited the trio to work at the station, mainly on weekends, to bring hip-hop onto the air. But it still wasn't part of the regular rotation.

"My challenge was a lot of those guys did excessive scratching," said Mayo. "They didn't talk. It was mostly playing the records. But they wouldn't play the whole thing through. When you're listening on the radio, that can be very disconcerting. The one person who ended up being the biggest of all those guys was Red Alert, because he focused more on playing more of the records. He wasn't somebody who overly mixed, and he had very good records. As opposed to focusing on the style, the technique."

In 1983, Mayo's Kiss 98.7 was locked in a battle with Crocker at WBLS. Bella arrived with Run-DMC's first single, "It's Like That."

"Barry, just put this record on the radio," Bella pleaded. "Play it once or twice. See what happens."

Mayo was not eager to play the single. It just wasn't his thing. He was a jazz and R&B guy. Music director Tony Quartarone, much younger and more connected to DJ culture, took up Bella's case. He told Mayo he was making a mistake. He pushed for "It's Like That." Tony Q, it turned out, was right.

"The response was crazy," Mayo said. "People just went nuts."

"The kids went out and bought the twelve-inch and slipped it over, and 'Sucker M.C.'s' was the bigger of the two in New York," said Bella. "Then the phones lit up. Barry was convinced 'This is how I'm going to beat Frankie Crocker.' From that day on, he started playing more and more rap records. Eventually, it became the number one radio station in New York."

Profile noticed. The first Run-DMC single hadn't been an immediate hit, but it quietly sold 25,000 copies. As soon as it entered the Kiss rotation, "that's when all hell broke out," said Plotnicki.

That led to Profile's next request. They wanted a Run-DMC album.

Russell Simmons first tried to push back. Another single would be fine. But a full record?

"I made them do it," said Robbins. "We had two hit twelve-inch singles. I said, 'I want you to make an album.' The guys and Russell were like, 'No, rap albums don't sell.' I said, 'Look, the contract says you have to make an album. You just need five more songs.'"

Chapter 6

AEROSMITH: JIMMY AND THE DOOF

He was lying there, the singer, and the lights were out. Face-down, covered by a mop of rock star hair.

They were in Portland, Maine, three weeks before Christmas 1979. At first, Jimmy Crespo, standing on the side, didn't notice, and kept playing. They were doing a song off the new record. This was supposed to be a moment of rebirth, reanimation, four gigs into the arrival of the new Aerosmith, *his* Aerosmith. Joe Perry might have been gone, but Jimmy Crespo was ready.

Brad Whitford walked over to Tyler, whose leg was twitching. He coolly gave him a soft kick, like he was testing out a set of Firestones. He walked over to Crespo, who had by that point abandoned "Reefer Head Woman."

"He's out," he told him.

"What do you mean he's out?" asked Crespo.

Under normal circumstances, or at least as normal a circumstance as might be found when your lead singer is facedown and you're going to have to tell thousands of fans to go home after three songs, you could at least hustle the singer out in the dark.

But Ron Pownall was usually prepared to document moments like this. Aerosmith's official photographer had his strobes hooked above the stage on the Cumberland County Civic Center's lighting truss. As the band's burly stage manager threw

Tyler over his shoulder, Pownall snapped a series of shots documenting the disaster.

The next day, Tyler called Crespo into his room.

He wanted him to know that this wasn't something that happened all the time. Don't get any weird ideas that this was what being in Aerosmith was going to be like.

"Okay, but for me, I had to look deep inside and decide what I wanted to do here," said Crespo. "You come to a crossroad. Which way do I go? Do I go back, do I stay? I somehow decided I should see it through. Whether it was the right thing to do or not, we'll never know."

• • •

How Crespo got into this pickle is no spy novel. The '70s had started as the band decade. Long-haired rock stars roamed the earth awash in cash, cocaine, and groupies. By the middle of the decade, they were playing festivals and arenas, smashing hotel rooms, and leaving trails of domestic dysfunction. Eventually, somebody or something had to shut down the party.

"Everyone was doing cocaine," said David Krebs, who began managing Aerosmith with Steve Leber in 1972. "If you're up at night and go to sleep, it's very hard to come down naturally. So they used heroin to bring them down and they would say, 'Don't worry, I've done this for years and it won't catch me.'"

Now they were junkies in a multibillion-dollar business dependent on new product, where there was barely time to take a breath. It was a snort, a gig, a party back at the hotel, a flight to Cleveland and do it again. The Eagles fell apart. Black Sabbath ditched Ozzy. Deep Purple lost Ritchie Blackmore. Little Feat.

Steely Dan. Led Zeppelin. All of them would dissolve during those years.

It had been a quick rise for Aerosmith. First record out in 1973. Douglas's arrival in 1974, kicking them from high school gyms to arenas. A critical and commercial peak in 1975 and 1976 with *Toys in the Attic* and *Rocks*.

Then 1977. That's when the rock star clichés caught up with them. Sports cars lined up outside the studio. The private plane. Huge houses, huge payrolls, huge drug habits. Nobody there to keep them in check.

Krebs, by now, was using.

"You lose that swing around power to say, 'It's okay to do cocaine and you can't do heroin,'" he said.

As the drugs took hold, the work suffered. When it came time to follow up *Rocks*, somebody cooked up a plan through which they would mobilize a toasted Aerosmith. They would strip away the distractions. They would take them away from the city, away from home.

This would not be the first time somebody thought that they could fix the complicated, combustible dysfunction within the group by simply changing the scenery. This would also not be the first time it proved futile.

In this case, Aerosmith rented the Cenacle, a huge former convent in rural New York, to make *Draw the Line*. One band under one roof. Until the drug dealers arrived. And the band started arguing. And everybody realized they were too burned out, stoned, or disinterested to get much of anything done. On a rare, good day, Douglas could coax Tyler out of his room to write a chorus or a verse. Most days were not good days.

The evidence is etched in vinyl. *Draw the Line* is the only Aerosmith record on which Douglas gets four writing credits and Whitford helped not only pen one of the only memorable tracks, "Kings and Queens," but he played both rhythm and lead guitar on the song. Tyler and Perry's partnership, meant to mirror Mick and Keith, resulted in just three cowrites.

Draw the Line would be a hit, rising to number eleven, but a much smaller hit than anybody expected. It would also mark the first step back. You could ignore that for a while, pretend it was just an aberration, not a trend. They were headlining the Texxas Jam, and cast on the big screen in Robert Stigwood's big-budget *Sgt. Pepper's Lonely Hearts Club Band*. But *Draw the Line* was more than a misstep. It was muddy, unfocused, and, if not quite "a truly horrendous record" as *Rolling Stone* magazine declared, it was certainly the first Aerosmith album that wasn't remotely as good as its predecessor.

The solution? Naturally, they got rid of Douglas. But that was just the first step.

• • •

There was, on paper, a fantastic, made-for-TMZ drama that happened on that July day in 1979, and with a headline to kill for: "Aerosmith Breaks Up Over Spilled Milk." And it is technically correct. A tiff between Elissa Perry and Terry Hamilton did occur backstage and was punctuated by the guitarist's wife tossing a calcium-rich glass of liquid at the bassist's wife.

But Aerosmith's collapse was already well under way. Joe Perry blames the drugs.

"I remember it as being just a progressive thing," said Perry.

"It's insidious. It creeps up on you. If you listen to some tapes of our live shows, you can start to hear it encroaching. It's a slow decline."

Aerosmith fell apart for the same reason almost every band does. The tension that sparks so much creativity can be tolerated, even celebrated, when you're young, hungry, and have everything to gain. That tension becomes a millstone when you're stars. You begin to believe you can do it alone, that you don't need all of the baggage that comes with carrying on this musical brotherhood. The death usually takes place in public, with thousands watching, internal squabbles turned into the performance itself. Phil Everly smashing his guitar and storming off the stage he shared with brother, Don. Glenn Frey, captured on the mic, threatening Don Felder as the Eagles come apart. Paul Simon recording a comeback record with Art Garfunkel and then, after a spat, stripping his musical partner's vocals off the tracks. After it's over, the forensic team moves in.

"You remember the movie *Rashomon*?" said Krebs. "It's about a murder. There were eight or nine witnesses. Every witness had a different recollection. That's what a rock and roll band's story is, especially after time passes."

The spilled-milk show does provide a window into just how unpleasant life in Aerosmith had become. They came to Cleveland's Lakefront Stadium as superstars, the headliners of an event called the World Series of Rock. They were to follow AC/DC, Journey, Thin Lizzy, Ted Nugent, and the Scorpions. The night before, Aerosmith stopped by WMMS, the city's influential FM station. John Gorman, the veteran program director, was working on the station's plans for the festival. He popped his head into an office and saw Tyler, on all fours, "snorting a line of cocaine that looked long enough to be a mile marker," he later wrote.

The next day would be no better. By then, lyric sheets would be taped all over the stage for Tyler.

"Aerosmith had gone from being a band that we were proud of, that made every show, to a band we could never be sure if we were going to cancel the next show," said Krebs. "It took me a long time to figure that out."

Photographer Bob Wallin, holding his Canon AE-1, had fond memories of Aerosmith live, dating back to a killer bill with Montrose five years earlier. This time, Wallin didn't like what he saw as he peered through his zoom. Tyler looked sloppy and wasted. He screwed up the intro to "Back in the Saddle," forcing the band to start over. Three times. Then he fell. Perry didn't look smashed.

"But you could see the look on his face," said Wallin. "Pissed and disgusted."

If anything, the backstage brawl over the milk seemed to bring Tyler back to life. He got right in the middle, shouting that Perry needed to get control of his woman. The guitarist walked out. He was never one to side with band over woman, not now, not ever. Everybody figured Perry would be back—until he wasn't.

• • •

Joe Perry had no exit plan.

"He didn't even tell me he had decided to move on for a couple of weeks after that whole thing went down," said Elissa Perry. "I just knew he was very angry."

"It was kind of like, things had reached a point where they were fed up with me and I was fed up with them, but I wasn't going to leave," said Perry. "And then I got away from them for a while and I started thinking about it."

Krebs had mixed feelings. He didn't want to lose Perry. But he was a Tyler guy. He and the singer spoke every day. He barely talked to Perry. As he contemplated how to save Aerosmith, he believed that separating the Toxic Twins might be his only hope.

"They both had heavy heroin problems," he said. "I really felt that if I only concentrated on Steven, maybe I could cure one without the other."

That Krebs decided to manage the post-Aerosmith Perry created its own complications. The guitarist had grown resentful of the manager, particularly after Krebs called a band meeting, before that last tour, to let each member know what they owed him for hotel-room-service bills. The other guys had run up tabs in the $10,000 range. Perry, Krebs told them, was $80,000 in the red.

Cash from the solo deal would help Perry pay back his managers. Hence, the Joe Perry Project. It's a perfect name for a band formed with such a vague sense of intention. *Project.* More like a school assignment than a future. Decades later, as a cleaned-up elder statesman of rock and roll, Perry would form a celebrity band with Johnny Depp, solo on an Eminem track, even play gigs with Pitbull. But the Project was the anti-supergroup. Perry hired Ralph Morman, a guy working construction at the time, to be his singer. David Hull, a journeyman who had recorded with the Dirty Angels, would play bass. He found drummer Ronnie Stewart working in a music store in Boston. So long, Cotton Bowl.

The Project played their first gig in the student union at Boston College.

Krebs wasn't impressed by Morman. He also wasn't surprised.

"I think what you're talking about is behavior called post-Tyler syndrome," he said. "Perry did not want to work with a strong singer this time around. So he didn't. He worked with a weak singer."

That said, the first JPP record has its moments. Douglas came back to produce, and "Let the Music Do the Talking," the lead single and title track, featured a driving slide riff and a strong hook. The record got solid reviews and sold a respectable 400,000 copies. It also allowed Perry to feel liberated from Aerosmith and from the normal power structure of a rock band. When Morman started acting up on the first tour, Perry simply fired him and brought in another singer, Charlie Farren. There would be no LSD—lead singer disease—in the Project.

"It felt like a big weight was lifted off my shoulders and it felt like I was in control again," Perry said. "Aerosmith had gotten to be so big and unmanageable for me. If we had had more of our wits about us we would have taken a year off and not broken the band up. But we didn't go that way."

If Perry felt relief, Tyler felt something else. Rejection, resentment, anger. He was the lead singer of Aerosmith, the greatest rock band in America. Joe Perry was his brother, his foil, his Keef. How could he leave that behind? This may as well have been the apartment at 1325 Commonwealth Avenue all over again.

"I remember thinking, 'Fuck you,'" said Tyler. "And I got replacements."

• • •

Michael Schenker was probably the most ridiculous to audition. With his Fabioesque mane of hair and Flying V guitar, the German-born axman looked better suited for *Lord of the Rings* than to roam the country with a group of hungover rock has-beens. Richie Supa made more sense. He and Tyler were close, and Supa had written "Chip Away the Stone," a staple in Aerosmith's sets. He also was deep into heroin, another activity for sharing. But Supa had another band and was under contract. So he gave the guys a tip. There was this guy, Jimmy Crespo, a guitarist whose own band had opened for him once.

"He was a small-town Long Island, local-bar-band guy who had great chops and the long, straight, dark, rock and roll look," said Supa. "Good look and would fit right in. He had that vibe, and he could play."

Could he play. He wasn't dangerous or unpredictable, like Perry.

"But he was really a great guitar player," said Douglas. "I mean, far better than anybody else that had been in that band. Technically, Crespo had it over everybody."

"Crespo came in with all the bullets in the chamber," said Tyler. "We never had a guitar player play with that kind of technique."

Technique. A word you'll hear over and over when Crespo's name comes up. Like it's a dirty word. As if Jimmy already had a strike against him. He was too good.

"Aerosmith didn't get together to be great musicians," Tyler said in the next breath. "We wanted to be a great band together."

Crespo actually didn't look much like Perry in person. From the crowd, though, and after shotgunning a few cans of Coors Light, they may as well have been twins. Dark shoulder-length hair that fell in front of his eyes. Wiry thin. He even played a Strat.

"Jimmy was a fucking amazing guitar player," Kramer said.

But that didn't mean he would fit in. Because Kramer began to realize he wouldn't.

"It was just difficult," said Kramer. "Aerosmith is that kind of thing. It's an apple pie. You can't take a piece of apple pie out of an apple pie and put a piece of blueberry in to replace it."

Crespo didn't fly in blind. Friends warned him about Aerosmith, that he was too nice for those guys. That they were out of their minds. But really, was he going to turn down a slot to play lead guitar for the American Stones? He loved *Toys in the Attic* and *Rocks*. As a kid, he'd run through those records in clubs. One thing Crespo didn't understand is the depth of the drug problems. He drank a little. He wasn't a junkie.

"I didn't know that Steven Tyler was a heroin addict," Crespo said. "These were party animals. Hard-core party animals. Heavy drugs. And partying all night, all day for a few days. All the guys. I don't care what anybody says. I was kind of the outsider. One time, they invited me to their suite, and every possible drug you could imagine was out there. Laid out on the table. And it was just party time. I couldn't believe it. I just said, 'Wow.' The next thing I knew, Steven was getting arrested or thrown out of the hotel because him and his wife were fighting. That's not a good sign."

Crespo did try. He started by jumping into the much-delayed sixth Aerosmith record.

Perry had still been in the band in the spring of 1979 when they entered the studio to record *Night in the Ruts*. The idea had been to finish the record and head out on the summer tour. But the sessions dragged on, with Tyler struggling to write. Instead of promoting a new album, the summer tour ended up as a way to raise more cash to pay for additional recording time.

By the time Aerosmith got back into the studio, post-Cleveland, new producer Gary Lyons had a band without a lead guitarist. Joe Perry's parts would remain on five songs. Supa filled in on two, and Crespo played lead on "Three Mile Smile." He was also featured alongside Whitford when the band lip-synched for two promo films. But clearly, there were still hopes Perry would return. When *Night in the Ruts* came out, on November 1, 1979, the Blue Army may have been comforted by the band photo on the cover. It featured Tyler, Perry, Whitford, Hamilton, and Kramer. They wore baggy clothes and makeup smeared on their faces to resemble dirt, as if they were emerging from a coal mine. The only problem is that the photo had been taken in 1978.

Ruts was better than *Draw the Line*, but not by much. It also didn't reverse the momentum. The record was certified as platinum, selling a million copies, half as many as *Draw the Line*.

The tour came next. At least the dates they could squeeze in. The Portland collapse, four shows into Crespo's tenure, would be a blip compared to what came next. In January 1981, Tyler, who had been drinking, hopped on a dirt bike in New Hampshire. He crashed. Crespo went to see him in the hospital.

"It was terrible," he said. "His heel came off. It was stuck in the chain. So that was when I decided, I've got to start writing stuff for him to listen to and to write to."

Though Crespo is treated as just a footnote in Aerosmith's history, he, in fact, lasted five years in the band. That's as long as Mick Taylor played with the Stones. But during that time, as hard as Crespo worked to leave his mark, there would be no *Let It Bleed*, *Sticky Fingers*, or *Exile on Main St.* on his résumé. It is Crespo who gets the bulk of the credit for the lone record that came out during his tenure, 1982's *Rock in a Hard Place.* Maybe, for a time, he was saving the band. The question is what band he was saving.

"The band wasn't the band without Joe," said Douglas, who was brought back from exile to try to salvage the post-Perry Aerosmith. "It was a different band. It was like Tom and Joey in a band with Crespo."

That actually became a possibility at one point. With Tyler in the hospital, Kramer suggested they start another band. He, Crespo, Hamilton, and a singer named Marge Raymond founded Renegade. They recorded together, but couldn't get a deal. And then Tyler, at least a vastly diminished Tyler, returned to regroup Aerosmith. If Perry wasn't there physically, he remained a force in absentia.

"Literally, Steven told me to just play the stuff that Joe did like he did and then do your own thing," said Crespo. "But all the roadies and everyone, they thought of Joe as a god. And I was always looked upon as, eh, so what that you could play better. Joe's the guy. I knew that I was stepping into a situation that was one of those you can't win. You're replacing the main character. You're replacing Keith Richards. How do you do that? You don't."

"They told him to be Joe," Douglas said. "They even put the

holster on him. That was terrible. It was like a disguise. The poor guy couldn't be himself."

If making *Draw the Line* and *Night in the Ruts* had been difficult, *Rock in a Hard Place* was like scaling an ice wall in bare feet. They burned through producers, endless hours, and about $2 million—at a time when tickets to see the Who could sell for $12.50. Money and time were not all they lost. They also lost another part of Aerosmith's core.

Whitford soldiered on through the sputtering attempts to tour in 1979 and 1980. The sessions for *Rock in a Hard Place* became too much.

"It was pretty obvious that something was not happening," he said. "When I got to the studio every day and it was me and Joey and Tom and Jimmy, and Steve, you know, if he did come, would never leave the lounge and a lot of times was just unable to even get up off the chair."

Whitford started a project with former Ted Nugent front man Derek St. Holmes. They recorded their self-titled debut in weeks, not months. One day, he found himself at Boston's Logan Airport with a flight to New York to do another Aerosmith session.

"I got as far as the airport and it felt so awful," he said. "I was in the airport and I got on the phone with David Krebs and I said this is physically messing me up. I can't do this."

• • •

The *Rock in a Hard Place* sessions started with producer Tony Bongiovi, the older brother of future feather-haired superstar Jon Bon Jovi. Eventually, the band brought Douglas back—a deeply damaged Douglas. In 1979, he had been hired by John

Lennon to produce his comeback record, *Double Fantasy*. The project had been a dream, working late nights with his hero on a record that would ultimately be a huge smash. But Lennon's death, on a cold night in December 1980, came only minutes after the former Beatle had left the studio and made breakfast plans with Douglas.

He became addicted to sleeping pills, and not long after, slipped into heroin addiction. One of the most successful record producers and talent scouts of the 1970s virtually disappeared. And *Rock in a Hard Place*, as flawed a record as it became, was his last real project for more than a decade.

Douglas's biggest contribution, early on, was to bring in the Doof. Whether that was a good idea or not remains up for debate.

Rick Dufay, veteran guitarist, had made a solo record, *Tender Loving Abuse*, with Douglas in 1980. He had also been institutionalized a few years earlier, diagnosed with schizophrenia. He got out of the psych ward by jumping out a window and breaking his ankle. The lithium kept him alive. It didn't destroy the Doof, though.

"He had the look, he could play anything they threw at him, and he totally had the attitude of not giving a shit," said Douglas.

Dufay did not come quietly. He didn't like Aerosmith, he told Douglas. He thought Perry was overrated, and this band he was being asked to audition for wasn't even Aerosmith.

"They sucked," Dufay said. "They were guys trying to survive. There wasn't anything musical about it. They were pissed off at Steven and pissed off at Joe because he abandoned them."

In his audition, Tyler asked him what Aerosmith songs he knew. He suggested they play "Walk This Way." Dufay told him he didn't know any of their songs. Tyler picked up the phone to call Douglas.

"I grabbed the phone from Steven's hand and said, 'What the fuck is the problem? It's obviously about your personality and dealing with you. I'm the biggest fucking pain in the ass in your life,'" said Dufay. "The other two guys heard all this shit and they started smiling. Because all these guys worshipped him. Steven and I yelled at each other for a few minutes and he said, 'I heard the album Jack did with you.' We played a couple songs and they were kind of shitty and then we started jamming a bit. Crespo's still on the other side of the stage. And then Steven starts singing. And I go, 'Oh, I see.'"

The Doof took some getting used to.

"I hated him at first because he was such an asshole," said Kramer. "He didn't give a shit about anything. He really couldn't play that good. He looked great. But it was all about his sense of humor, and it took me a while to get it. He wasn't a serious enough musician for me, but I will say, when it came down to it, we did end up being very good friends."

Crespo didn't come around.

"He was really crazy," he said. "He'd eat a cockroach just to make a scene. That kind of stuff. And that's the way it was all the time with him. There was always this hyper, crazy energy coming from him. I guess it was just to sidetrack Steven. But it wasn't helping."

For Kramer, Dufay did bring something that had been missing: the chemistry of being in a gang. Perry, so detached, hadn't provided that. Nor could Crespo, who was so tightly wound.

"For me, that's what being in a band was all about," Kramer

said. "When I watched the Beatles when I was fourteen years old on Ed Sullivan, it wasn't Ringo that attracted me to it, and it wasn't the drums that attracted me to do it. It was the camaraderie of what these guys were doing together. And that's what I had with Rick. He was into it and he was into being part of the band."

Some band. The guitarists were brand-new and shared only one bond, a brooding dislike for each other. The bassist and drummer, with their own drug problems, were trying to survive, even if they knew it would never work. Then there was the leader. That Steven Tyler even made it to a microphone during this period is stunning.

They weren't going to be able to make it work in a regular studio setting. So Douglas tried an old trick. He moved the recording to another location. He set up Tyler in a resort in Florida on Sonesta Beach. He rented a mobile studio and parked it outside. That way Tyler wouldn't have to hustle far beyond his front door to lay down his vocals.

Somebody needed to stay with Tyler, to watch over him, to at least try to help him get straight. The Doof to the rescue.

"That defined their relationship more than anything," said Douglas. "Because he really took care of him. They slept in the same bed sometimes because Steven would be shaking and cold. 'Rick, I'm cold.'"

It wasn't pretty. Dufay estimates Tyler fired him four or five times during his tenure. Sometimes, he got no farther than the lobby before Tyler ran down to get him, pleading that he come back. One tantrum found the singer, who had been guzzling methadone to maintain, dumping the little bottles into the toilet. Douglas happened to be there that day. He turned to Dufay.

"That's very bad," he said. "He's going to get very sick."

Dufay did his best.

"Tom Hamilton would make a gram of coke last a fucking week, but he would always have it on him," said Dufay. "Joey Kramer was a coke head, too. And booze. But nothing like Steven. He's got the constitution of a fucking ox. When we were in the hotel, he would go into convulsions and scare the shit out of me. I would have to put him in the bathtub and run water on him. He'd say, 'What the fuck are you doing?' I'd say, 'You were having a seizure.'"

Another time, they went outside to get some sun.

"We get into the stall and he said, 'I've got a two-gram vial in my bathing suit.' I snorted half of it. He snorted the other half. And we walk across the whole pool area. As soon as we hit the pool area, he's straightened up like nothing is wrong. As soon as we get to the elevator, he collapsed. I carried him up to the room and put him to bed."

Rock in a Hard Place did eventually get finished. It is not a terrible record. There are songs on it—a cover of "Cry Me a River," for one—that feature Crespo playing in ways nobody had played on an Aerosmith record before. In all, the guitarist got writing credit on seven of ten songs.

But *Rock* sold sparingly upon its release in August 1982, stopping at number thirty-two on the *Billboard* charts, and its only hit, "Lightning Strikes," was a minor hit at best. The real problem was that the album's failure didn't seem to be much of a wake-up call.

Douglas went to see Aerosmith in the fall of 1983.

In the dressing room, he could tell Tyler was messed up.

Steven started pleading with Douglas to go onstage and sing backup.

"I said, 'Steven, I'm not in the band,'" said Douglas. "Steven says, 'That's why I want you to wear a dress.' He wanted me to come out in a dress. No one will know it's me."

That night, Tyler couldn't sing. He would wave the mic at the audience, asking them to fill in the words. Then he was done, flat-out, passed out. Joe Baptista, the road manager, again at the mic, let the crowd know. The jig was up.

Chapter 7
RUN-DMC: LONGPLAY, WITH GUITARS

The beauty is how little was at stake. There were no rap superstars, no Jay Z, Dr. Dre, or even Hammertime. All you had was a small misunderstood subculture and a mainstream America that barely knew it existed. Sometimes, the music historians will bring up the Sugarhill Gang banging to the beat on *Soul Train*, or Debbie Harry, bare-shouldered and awkwardly dropping Flash's name, and yes, these technically were raps, but they may as well have been "Monster Mash." Novelty songs. They certainly didn't change a single radio station's playlist.

Nobody, in 1983, made a rap record thinking it might lead to a career in music.

That's the context as Larry Smith and Russell Simmons gathered at Greene St. Recording in the heart of SoHo. The lack of stakes was freeing. The only limits were financial, and those limits, looking back, helped more than hurt. Even if somebody wanted to slather Run's and D's raps with a thick rhythm section and *Saturday Night Fever*-ish orchestrations, they simply couldn't afford to. That's particularly important to note when you read an interview Smith gave, almost twenty years later, to hip-hop historian Brian Coleman.

"If I had had the budget," he said, "I would have hired live performers on the whole first Run-DMC album."

Sugar Hill did that. The Robinsons had enough cash to bring

in a house band with some of the finest funk players in the business. They could take Chic or Liquid Liquid and re-create their best songs as a backing track, note for note. Which is why the Treacherous Three, so dangerously hot at Harlem World, became a glorified disco band on record.

For Run-DMC, Smith couldn't even afford to use Orange Krush. What had been a band became, in Smith's words, "a philosophy." At Greene St., the band was Smith and a bass, an Oberheim DMX drum machine, and a Prophet-5 keyboard.

There are a few misconceptions about how that first album came together. One is that Jay was intricately involved. The record did, after all, include the songs "Jam-Master Jay" and "Jay's Game." In reality, Jay wouldn't become an official member of Run-DMC until after the record, when they needed a DJ. And even then he would remain technically a sideman by contract for years, official in every way except for on paper. The guys split up their tour money evenly, but Jay's record royalty cut was smaller. "Why do you think Jay was never on the cover?" said DMC. "Profile would not allow Jay to be on the cover. We made them put Jay on the back of the album."

There is also the false idea that Smith was the music man and Simmons the business mogul. It's true that Russell couldn't so much as play "Chopsticks" on the Prophet, but what he offered, as far as musical direction, was vital in its own way.

"Larry was the genius in the studio," said drummer Trevor Gale, a member of Orange Krush when it had been an active band. "Larry was the guy who said, 'Play four bars, stop on the fifth bar, come back in on the fourth bit of the fifth bar.' Russell was the guy that was there that said, 'I don't like how that feels.

Make it sound like mashed potato with gravy on it.' Larry could write out a chart, but Russell would definitely contribute from an almost spiritual, emotional, feeling energy. 'Make it sound street, make it sound rough.' It was very important."

Simmons operated with what he called "an unwritten rule."

"We would never use instrumentation that was on any R&B record," he said. "All that Shalamar and shit. We hated that."

To hear Russell tell it, the stripped-down sound was a strategy, not a cost-cutting measure. Later, he might be scoring the cover of *Businessweek* as the mogul who turned hip-hop into an industry, but it still bugs Simmons that he didn't get writing credit for "Sucker M.C.'s," even though the beat came straight from "Action," which he did get writing credit for.

"That was my beat," he said. "Larry took credit, but that was my beat."

Simmons broke down his working relationship with Smith without hesitation.

"Larry's a jazz, R&B guy," he said. "You're taking a jazz, R&B guy and you're stripping him down. 'Don't play too much, Larry. Don't put too many layers of instrumentation on it. Let's take this and repeat it eighty-four times.' He wanted to play. He's a musician. But he had a great sense of melody and he understood B-boy music. He was able to get the feeling from hanging out in the Fever. I took him to all the hip-hop clubs. And he fell in love with it."

Run-DMC's self-titled debut has been overshadowed by the critical and commercial smash of *Raising Hell* and even the group's less-explosive second album, *King of Rock*. It's no different from how *Meet the Beatles!* is often ignored for the studio wizardry that stretches from *Revolver* and *Sgt. Pepper* to *Abbey Road*. But when you actually drop the needle on the Beatles' debut, you get a startling reminder of the raw power as those two C chords slide into a D and the Mersey Beat blasts out of your speakers. "I Want to Hold Your Hand." "I Saw Her Standing There." "All My Loving." So upfront, so full of energy, so urgent. Such is the case with Run-DMC's first album.

Start with the singles.

"It's Like That" arrived on November 1, 1983. It's as bare as can be. A drumbeat, a few keyboard chords, hand claps. The only flourish may be the rolls across the tom-tom drums.

The B-side had even more impact. "Sucker M.C.'s" is what caught Rick Rubin's attention when he was a student at NYU trying to build his own label. You can follow the stylistic line from "Sucker" to Rubin's first Def Jam productions, both released the following year—T La Rock's "It's Yours" and LL Cool J's "I Need a Beat."

"Sucker" opens with seven hard beats, a cymbal, hand claps . . . and then everything drops out except those claps.

Two years ago, a friend of mine
Asked me to say some MC rhymes.

Run's rap, more than 124 seconds, delivers virtually every lyrical element that will define a genre of music.

There are the lifestyle brags ("champagne, caviar, and bubble bath"), put-downs ("You're a five-dollar boy and I'm a million-dollar man"), and the important meta-acknowledgment of sonic superiority ("Dave cut the record down to the bone"). And while Run blasts through the first two-thirds of "Sucker

M.C.'s," DMC pops in at 2:15 and carries it home for the last fifty seconds. Listening to DMC, it's clear why he quickly became the closer. His voice is deeper, his delivery harder. It is the voice of authority, gravitas, even when he's basically introducing himself with a name tag.

I'm DMC in the place to be
I go to St. John's University.

The second Run-DMC single, which arrived in December, was a cover of "Hard Times," a song first recorded by Kurtis Blow on his 1980 debut album. It barely resembles the original. On that, Blow discos his way through, shouting as he's headed to the bridge like James Brown. "It's getting funky now," he lets everybody know, and buries the hard tale of economic disparity in a dance groove. Run and D's rap don't dress up a beat. There's an occasional keyboard chord, but otherwise, "Hard Times" is as raw.

"Jam-Master Jay," on the B-side, is Rubin's other favorite off the first album. Which is telling. Run-DMC's debut opens with "Hard Times" and "Rock Box," but it's the last three songs on the side—"Jam-Master Jay," "Hollis Crew (Krush-Groove 2)" and "Sucker M.C.'s (Krush-Groove 1)"—that feature the sound that caught the producer's ear.

"I liked 'Sucker M.C.'s,' that was my favorite by far," said Rubin. "I liked 'Jam-Master Jay.' In many ways, I feel like those really were the first, maybe the first real hip-hop records. Before that, if you heard things like 'Christmas Rappin'' and records like that, those were not hip-hop records. Those were R&B records with rapping."

Which brought Rubin to a song he did not like on that first

record. His choice is as revelatory as what he loved. That song is "Rock Box."

"Rock Box" wasn't just Run-DMC's third single. It is the song that Run and D held up as their most innovative creation, much more than the collaboration with Tyler and Perry.

"The most revolutionary record I made isn't 'Walk This Way,'" said DMC. "The most revolutionary record I made is definitely 'Rock Box.'"

"I like 'Rock Box' ten times better than 'Walk This Way,'" added Run. "Twenty times."

Why?

"It's a better record," he said. "We made a black rock record. Ridiculously fly with echo chambers. 'Walk This Way' is a big, big hit, crossed over to people like you, because it came from a guy like Rick."

"Rock Box" had something you couldn't find anywhere else on the group's debut record or anywhere in hip-hop—a blistering guitar solo from Eddie Martinez. That's what Rubin takes issue with. He favored barre chords, grit, Black Sabbath over hair metal.

"It felt disingenuous to me as a rock record," he said. "The rock guitar seemed like someone who was not ensconced in rock music making a record with rock trappings. For me, 'Rock Box' didn't have the spirit of rock and roll in it."

Let's table that for a minute. Because it may be one of the rare times Rick Rubin was flat-out wrong.

"Rock Box" brought rock and rap together two years before

the Toxic Twins hustled into Manhattan. What separates it from "Walk This Way" is that it isn't a cover song done with a pair of famous white rock stars. It's Run-DMC with Martinez's flash.

"Rock Box" started as a song about weed.

"'Wheeling, dealing, you got a funny feeling,'" DMC quotes. "'You tried your best to smoke that sensi.'"

The first line stayed. The second got cut.

"Russell's like, 'You can't put out a record about weed.' So I changed the routine to write about rapping the house."

The lyrics are, in this case, really secondary. What's revolutionary is the sound.

"Rock Box" opens with just drums and Run's voice on deep echo, the delay pushed so much that it masks the fact that he's saying "fresh shit" and not just "fresh." In some places, the credits list Jay for the programmed drums, but DMC said he did them.

Smith knew he loved Billy Squier's song "The Big Beat," the opener on the power pop singer's 1980 debut. Those drums, played by Bobby Chouinard, would be one of the most sampled in rap history, grabbed by everyone from Run-DMC and Jay Z to Kanye. Smith pulled out the DMX drum machine, still relatively new—Oberheim introduced it in 1981—and gave DMC a quick lesson.

"He says, 'Here's the kick, here's the snare,' and he said, 'I'll cue it up for you,'" remembered DMC. "Boom, bam. Boom, boom bam. Boom, bam. Boom, boom bam."

Smith laid on the bass, keyboards, and bells.

Run and D left Greene St. for a while. That's when Smith called an old friend from the neighborhood into the studio. Martinez, just about to turn thirty, was the son of Puerto Rican immigrants and a seasoned session player who would go on to play on Robert Palmer's "Simply Irresistible," Meatloaf's "I'd Do Anything for Love (But I Won't Do That)," and Billy Ocean's "Suddenly." He was hot off a tour as Blondie's second guitarist.

"He played me the track," said Martinez. "Really, it was just a DMX drum machine and the bass guitar. I didn't feel it was odd. I felt it was interesting. And I liked it. It was very free. The track was so sparse that when I played on it, I just put a million guitars on it. You're adding music to make it larger."

Martinez put his red Hamer guitar through a Boss overdrive.

"It sounded like a moose," he said.

Run and D weren't quite as thrilled when they returned to the studio. Martinez was gone by the time Smith played it for them.

"You can't fuckin' hear the beat," Run complained. "The guitar is too loud."

• • •

"It sounds so normal to me now," said DMC. "But when we first heard it, that shit was like psychedelic drugs. 'Rock Box' was the first rock-rap record. Larry putting us over metal guitars. That's our fucking claim to fame. It wasn't a fucking remake. It had nothing to do with nothing. That's why Larry's the greatest hip-hop producer who ever lived."

Selling "Rock Box" became yet another headache for Manny Bella, Profile's radio promo man.

"Like pulling teeth," he said. "Nobody understood. 'Why are there freakin' rock guitars on this rap record?'"

Over at Kiss, Mayo, who had only reluctantly played "It's

Like That" and "Sucker M.C.'s" a few months earlier and been proven wrong, still wasn't about to take Bella on faith. He didn't like "Rock Box." He didn't want to play it.

"It was just an unnatural sound, those guitars mixed with hip-hop beats," he said. "It wasn't something that just felt right."

Bella tried everything. He even had Simmons get Smith to create a version of the song stripped of Martinez's lead. It didn't make much of a difference. While "Hard Times" and "It's Like That" cracked the R&B Top 20, "Rock Box" didn't chart.

Which is not to say that "Rock Box" failed to reach an audience. Plotnicki saw to that. He came up with a plan for breaking the song. By now, music videos were standard for any rock or pop star with chart aspirations. Rappers were a different story. Run-DMC would make a video for "Rock Box," a daring decision considering that a video ended up costing Profile $25,000, more than the cost of recording the entire album.

Not only that, but this was when MTV didn't play rap. The network barely played music by black artists. Critics would call it racism. MTV's execs would call it formatting. The music network followed the programming model of album-oriented rock radio, so as long as AOR was heavy on Def Leppard, Billy Joel, and Huey Lewis, so was MTV.

For their video debut, Run-DMC did not open with the DMX beat. The action kicked off with a monologue from Professor Irwin Corey, the then sixty-nine-year-old, white-haired comic who billed himself as the World's Foremost Authority on Everything.

"Now, what is rap music?" Corey asked before an almost impenetrable ramble meant as comic relief.

Plotnicki's other crossover attempt involved inserting a young white boy in the video whose primary role seems to be bringing a young white boy into Run-DMC's world. At one point, the boy exchanges a knowing wink with Jay.

It isn't until almost ninety seconds into the video that we hear Run's voice on the echoed opening and see Larry Smith's Cadillac roll up to the Danceteria.

Run-DMC encounters the kind of crowd you might find at the club, from B-boys with sweat suits to white girls in Madonna-inspired fishnet tank tops. Inside the club, Run-DMC takes the stage. Martinez and his guitar get a prime spot to the left side. Smith is in back, a giant *Larry* belt buckle on his jeans.

"Rock Box" has been billed as the first rap video played on MTV. That's certainly true. But as significantly, it introduced the public to the band's third member. He stood behind Run and D on the stage, danced, smiled, and clapped. He hadn't played on the actual recording of "Rock Box," but he was happy to synch along, because he would become a vital member of Run-DMC. Jason Mizell was now the DJ.

The response on black radio and in the black press may have been tentative at first. Not so in the white press.

Roy Trakin, in *Creem*, proclaimed that "Rock Box" "does for rap what Eddie Van Halen did for Michael Jackson—bringing it to a whole new audience." *Rolling Stone*, in its four-star review of Run-DMC's debut album, highlighted "Rock Box" for "melting rap into rock like it's never been done before." The *Village Voice*'s Pazz & Jop poll listed the single the seventh best of 1984, ahead of U2, R.E.M., and the Pretenders. By December, nine months after its release, Run-DMC's self-titled debut was certified gold, meaning it was the first rap record to sell more than 500,000 copies.

Reggie Osse, a fourteen-year-old kid in Brooklyn, wasn't watching the charts. He remembered hearing "Rock Box" for the first time on his JVC boom box.

"I was like, 'What the fuck is that?' It's the same guys that recorded 'Sucker M.C.'s,' but now there's this guitar riff and it just took hip-hop to a whole different level," he said.

Osse didn't think about whether it was the first rock-rap record or its role in the history of musical innovation. He contemplated those questions later as he moved out of the neighborhood to attend Cornell University, earned a law degree, and launched a career as a lawyer, then the editor of *The Source*, and finally as the pioneering podcaster Combat Jack. "I remember playing that record over and over, and once the video dropped, I couldn't get enough of it," he said during the summer of 2017, only months before he died of cancer at fifty-three. "It was like the rap gods delivered us the record we had never heard of."

Chapter 8

AEROSMITH: BOTTOM

If things were bad in Aerosmith, they weren't much better with the Project. The promise of the first record had devolved during a messy tour. Morman was fired, replaced by local rocker Charlie Farren. The band's second album, *I've Got the Rock 'n' Rolls Again*, barely sold. Columbia Records dropped Perry. So did manager Don Law, who had taken over the Project after Leber and Krebs. That's when Tim Collins entered the picture.

Whatever expectations there were, they were tempered by the fact that Collins had little experience and no clout. At twenty-seven, his only other real client was Jonathan Edwards, a folk singer a decade past his lone hit, a Vietnam-era protest song called "Sunshine." He at least had a degree from Bentley College, where he had majored in marketing and organizational behavior.

The first meeting with Perry did not go well. On a bitterly cold, rainy night in January, Collins met with Perry's band. Farren didn't like him and told Perry so. But a month later, the phone rang in Collins's office. Elissa Perry told him to come over to the house in Chestnut Hill.

He drove to the wealthy Boston suburb, walked in, and saw Perry holding their baby, Adrian. The baby started playing with Collins's bushy beard, which seemed to break the ice. Elissa turned to Collins. She told him he was now Perry's manager. Perry invited Collins into the den, and they stayed for hours.

"We snorted coke, drank whiskey, and talked about everything under the sun," said Collins. "That's how it started. He was essentially bankrupt. But he wasn't really bankrupt, because there were all types of funds connected to Aerosmith he wasn't getting paid."

Back in those days, Collins drank hard but hadn't crossed over into addiction. He kept it to the weekends. He knew that this was an incredible opportunity, with some key caveats. Perry was clearly on the wrong side of his drug habit. He and Elissa had a combustible relationship. This version of the Project was, at best, mediocre. But Collins wasn't an idiot. He knew that Aerosmith, together, was bigger than anything he could ever hope to sign. The band's greatest hits record, released in November 1980, would only need four months to be certified gold.

"I knew the first thing we had to do was get money and make a record deal in order to get him moving, and I had to clean up the situation with the band," he said.

Drummer Stewart was the only holdover from the original Joe Perry Project. Collins brought in Danny Hargrove to play bass. When Farren quit, he found Mark "Cowboy Mach" Bell to sing.

For Bell, this was no regular gig. Perry and Tyler were heroes. He had seen Chain Reaction, Tyler's pre-Aerosmith band, in New Hampshire. Now he would be playing alongside Perry.

Today, Bell teaches music to children with cognitive disabilities and remembers his days with the Project fondly. It may have been a low point for Perry, but for Bell it would be the closest he ever felt to being a rock star. There would be a record deal, international dates, and, on those rare nights when the band's namesake was properly medicated, real musical highs.

As such, Bell didn't let those days slip by without documentation. His date book marks the significant moments in the Project, starting with the Friday afternoon of February 23, 1982, when Bell drove up to the rehearsal room in Cambridge, Massachusetts, for the first time. He saw the Corvettes parked outside. He met Whitford, who was helping Perry out for a stretch, inside with the band. He was cordial, but quiet. Perry was standing in the corner. He wore tight leather pants and had luxuriant, huge hair. That was the good news.

"His skin looked vampirish, like greenish," Bell remembered. "He was incredibly thin and visibly shaking. Definitely ill and not right, but he could play. He's just knocking off these guitar riffs. Some of them I recognized from the Project, some from Aerosmith, some I didn't recognize at all. I had been given five songs to audition with the band. Brad said, 'Hey, what else do you know?' I say, 'How about some Jeff Beck? Some Yardbirds?' So we started doing 'I'm Not Talking,' 'Going Down,' different tunes. It seemed like everything I played, they knew."

With the new Project assembled, Collins had to get them some business. Perry had just taken a second mortgage out on his house. He was paying more than 30 percent in interest a year. It was a mess financially.

Then there was the matter of Elissa.

"People say he made her crazy," said Collins. "Other people

say she made him crazy. It didn't matter to me. I got the band together and got him out of there."

They headed out on tour in mid-May. Elissa, whether she wanted to come or not, would remain at home. This wasn't 1977. The Aerosmith plane was gone. Instead, Collins had borrowed a dingy Dodge van that Edwards owned. Road manager Doc McGrath took the wheel. Perry rode shotgun.

Whitford came along for the first round of gigs in 1982. Bell, still starstruck, picked his brain about Aerosmith, since Perry wouldn't discuss those days at all.

"We were doing like 'Toys in the Attic' and 'Same Old Song and Dance,'" Bell said. "There were certain ones they just wouldn't play. 'Dream On.' They had demonized Steven Tyler to the point in their minds that he was not mentioned, and they wouldn't do songs that were too much of a Steven Tyler production."

Whitford could step up and take his parts. But fewer than a dozen gigs in, he had to head to the West Coast for another project. That's when Perry began to falter.

Bell marked the lowest point in his datebook: May 17, 1982. Jacksonville, North Carolina.

"We're listening to Sex Pistols on the tape deck," said Bell. "We always listened to the Sex Pistols or AC/DC and we're just driving down the road and all of a sudden Joe's head shoots up toward the ceiling of the van and he stiffens like a board and he's vibrating and the veins on his edge are bulging and he looks like a Frankenstein monster. My heart stops, and as it's stopping, Ronnie Stewart, who is in the very back of the van, who has his headphones on and is whacking along on this pad, he rips off his headphones, flies over the bench seats, and as he's flying through the air, he's ripping his wallet out of his back pocket and jams his wallet into Joe's mouth. Either Ronnie had seen this earlier or Ronnie was trained as an EMT. I had never seen anything like it. The road manager swerves off the road. He's trying to calm down Joe. Joe is breathing hard, but he relaxes a bit and he said, 'We've got to get you to some kind of health stop and get you checked out.' Joe does not tell the doctor that he's a junkie, he doesn't tell the doctor that the pills or whatever paraphernalia in his bag were taken out. So the doctor's not able to make any real determination, except it seems like the worst is past."

They got back on the road and to a club, the Chateau Madrid. It was across from the local military base. They got onstage, and early in the set, Perry stepped up to the mic, went stiff again, and fell to the ground. A member of the road crew yanked Perry off stage, and the club owner came over to find out what was happening. Doc McGrath stepped in. He had a fit, telling him the sound system was screwed up and had given Perry a shock.

"Your sound system's fucked up, man," McGrath yelled. "You just shocked our headliner. You might have killed him."

Of course, if the club owner knew what had really happened, he wouldn't have paid the Project.

Looking back, Joe Perry did not describe those days as doomed.

"I understand why so much weight gets put on how fucked up you were, but I was doing what I wanted to do," he said. "I wanted to get out on the road and get away and do what I do best and love to do. Which is play. But I've got to say, it felt good."

They met Bo Diddley and Chuck Berry on that road trip. They tried to hitchhike from Huntington Beach to L.A.—nobody would pick them up—until they could hop a bus. They visited the Lincoln Memorial in D.C. It was an adventure, stuff he had never done with Aerosmith.

Perry remembered the seizure and insisted it had nothing to with drugs.

"I had stopped doing dope and even coke because I didn't have the money," he said. "I was drinking. That's about it. I was up a couple nights straight. I wasn't exactly eating right. I remember checking in with a doctor and he said, 'Go home and get some sleep and some steak.'"

Chapter 9

RUN-DMC: JAY

Early in 1985, Tim Sommer did a long interview with Russell Simmons for *Heavy Metal*, a magazine known for its bizarre combination of top-notch science fiction writing and erotic cartoons. Looking back, the two-page spread is fascinating for several reasons.

In the intro, Sommer notes that he was cruising around with "my friend Rick" on a run for White Castle burgers the first time he heard "Rock Box." He mentions that Rick is "a volume and beat fanatic" whose powerful car sound system had been installed by DJ Jazzy Jay. What Sommer doesn't mention is Rick's last name. It's Rubin.

Fourteen months later, Rick Rubin would be deified the King of Rap by the *Village Voice*—a bearded, sonic shaman with two killer production credits: LL Cool J's debut, *Radio*, and *Raising Hell*. In Sommer's piece, he might as well be Barry Rubin.

The next revelation concerns the presentation of Run-DMC. The *Heavy Metal* issue was coming out on the cusp of the release of *King of Rock*, but from the way he wrote, it's clear Sommer hadn't been given an advance copy. He doesn't actually even mention the record. Instead, he talks about Run-DMC's debut and also about what Simmons, in unsparing terms, called the main barrier to the group's emergence as superstars.

Hint: It wasn't white people. The racism holding Run-DMC back, he said, came from the black community.

"They don't understand it," Simmons told Sommer. "I'd like to think that's the most important reason. But it's also not sophisticated enough for them. They're bourgeois blacks. The guys remind them of the corner, and they came from there, and they're away from there now. They want to be as far from that as they can be. It's street. It's too black for them."

The truly notable part of this interview is who was not mentioned. Jam Master Jay. A photograph doesn't even include him. It shows Simmons sitting next to Run and D. In his intro, Sommer references DJ Run. In a world still not all that familiar with Run-DMC, it wouldn't be hard to imagine many readers assuming Run is the MC *and* behind the turntables.

The omission is actually no surprise. Remember, Profile didn't allow the group to put Jay on the album covers, only showing Run and D. Yet Jay was anything but a bit player. The cliché, years later, would be to call him the glue. At the least, in those days, he was as important to his group as the drummer and bassist in a classic rock power trio. He would also become more than the rhythm section. As time passed, as Run and Darryl continued to goof off, smoke weed, and suck down Olde English, Jay would be sitting at the board, watching how Larry Smith and later Rubin turned rhymes into fully realized recordings. This focus came as no surprise to Jeff Fludd, his high school buddy and later Run-DMC's road manager. It made perfect sense.

"DJs transform into producers," said Fludd. "It's quite natural, because you have an ear for sound."

In the studio, Jay became invaluable by the time Run-DMC

recorded *Raising Hell*. He was the bridge between the board and the guys, the voice of reason and the badass who could focus D on the task at hand and call Run "a fat motherfucker" without ruffling his ego. He could get two MCs—high on forties and french fries—to focus enough to lay down their raps. By the end, it would be hard to imagine that this man, so focused and disciplined, was actually a few months younger than his partners.

The greatest marker of Jay's central role is what happened after he was gone. He was shot in 2002 in his recording studio, a murder that remains unsolved. And Run-DMC effectively fell apart as a touring entity. After that, Jam Master Jay would be recognized for the multiple roles he served: protector, tastemaster, peacemaker, and taskmaster.

"Jay was the backbone," said Jeff Townes, who, as DJ Jazzy Jeff, would form a magical duo with his friend Will Smith. "Run-DMC were the superstars, and Jay was the unofficial leader of Run-DMC."

• • •

If there is one thing that set them apart, it is where they came from. Joey and Darryl were Hollis from the start. It wasn't Beverly Hills, but this section of Queens was defined by its middle-classness—the neat lawns, the fences, the paved driveways. You knew the dodgy spots and could avoid them. Jay was from Brooklyn, all the way, even after making his great escape to Hollis as a boy. The projects were more than a memory.

"He had the Brooklyn in him," said Marvin Thompson, his stepbrother, who was ten years older. "You don't get rid of that.

You born with that. It's called survival. You get down or you lay down."

Those roots didn't just make him more street savvy. They made Jay more serious, all about taking care of the business.

Danny Simmons always found himself drawn to Jay, sometimes more than to his younger brothers. They tended to be protected and sheltered by their parents. Jay's hunger made him appealing.

"Run later became a TV star, but Jay, early on, was like, 'This is my opportunity,'" said Danny. "Joey would have been fine no matter what. He would have been a college kid, middle-class, living in Hempstead, with a wife and three kids. Jay saw this as an opportunity for a lot of different things, and he treated it as such. Jay was like, 'This shit fell in my lap and I'm going to make the most of it.'"

Like his future musical partners, Jay came from a good home. Connie Mizell taught kindergarten and first grade. Jesse Mizell was a social worker at the welfare office. The two had met at Marvin's Boy Scout troop in Brooklyn. (Marvin never knew his father.) Jason William Mizell, their son, arrived on January 21, 1965.

They were more than lucky to get to Hollis. As Marvin tells it, sometime before Jason's tenth birthday, a friend from their church in Brooklyn—who lived in Hollis—told Connie about a house for sale across the street. The Mizell family didn't have a car. They took the J train to Queens to see the modest home on 203rd Street. Marvin couldn't believe it. No sharing a stairwell with a passed-out junky. The Mizells would have their own space.

For a group of kids, Queens had everything, from the playground hoops to the crews on the corner. For a group of aspiring musicians, Queens also had mystique. In the early part of the twentieth century, it became a refuge for black musicians kept out of the lily-white suburbs. Louis Armstrong, Dizzy Gillespie, and Ella Fitzgerald all called Queens home. Later, it would spawn a generation of hip-hop stars from LL Cool J to Ja Rule, the park jams filled with turntables.

Those streets inspired Run and D without swallowing them. They watched, took mental notes, and stayed out of trouble.

"You have a choice when you live in a lower-middle-class neighborhood," said Russell Simmons. "You can go to the corner. People on the corner are in gangs and selling drugs. Jay had Hollis Avenue in him. Jay had the corner in him. D went to Catholic school, so he was different. But the Hollis Crew—Jay's friends, our friends, the younger brothers of my friends—they were always around them, so they were surrounded by the elements. A lot of the poets write songs about their friends. They wrote about being tough enough to hang in the street, but not being stupid enough to follow the street."

"Jay was tough," said DMC. "He was in the street. Jay was the dude that wouldn't let the bullies take the money from the kids when he was around. He wasn't going to let you fuck with people that he knew. When we put Jay in the group, the reason we were so happy was the Hollis Crew was with Jay, so now we had three bodyguards."

Run does believe there are a few perceptions about Hollis that have been distorted over the years. Start with the portrayal of his home neighborhood as a kind of war zone, a gangland you couldn't walk through without being robbed or beaten.

"First of all, I went to Hollis every day," he said. "Let's get it correct. Played basketball at 192 Park. I walked by myself to Hollis, to go get my White Castle burgers and go watch the Hollis bitties inside 192. I'm not going to create for you tremendous fear."

Was there crime? Sure. Did his babysitters tell him, as a boy, not to go out after five? Definitely. That doesn't mean it was South Central.

"When you're born somewhere, you just hear what not to do by the elders of the town and you don't do it," he said. "But then, you know, even when I went to go get Darryl every day when I've discovered 197th street, I wouldn't go down Hollis Ave. I'd go down 104th street; 104th street's kind of calm."

Jeff Fludd has a term for the kids who did that, who stayed off Hollis Avenue. They were "backstreet cats." They operated that way out of experience and necessity.

"It's just like the guy who walks down the street and there's a big hole," he said. "The first time he fell into it. The next time he walked around it. The next time he walked around the corner."

Jay had always been into music. Ryan Thompson, a friend later known as DJ Doc, remembered seeing him playing drums in a band as a kid and, as a teenager, rolling down Jefferson Street in Brooklyn during a parade. Jay worked the bongos on a float and "he tore it up."

In the early days, when they needed more protection, Jay served that role. Not to physically beat anybody down, but just to keep Run and D safe by making it clear that they were his boys.

Jay was definitely there to "keep the wolves at bay, the bullies off Run-DMC," said Thompson. "But he was also serious about music. Jason really cared about these two men. These are cool guys. He knew they were different from him, but they were cool guys and he recognized their talent."

The Hollis Crew wasn't so much a gang, Thompson explains. But they did offer strength in numbers.

"We were a crew of individuals who hang out, play basketball, chase the young girl type of thing," he said. "We wasn't a gang in that we wanted to go out and fight other gang members. If there were any problems, definitely we'd defend ourselves."

To Run's point, in Hollis you could live in peace, but you also always needed to be watching your back. In that spirit, Jay was the perfect addition to Run-DMC.

"When I say street cred, I mean protector," said Run. "Running with Jay, nothing gonna happen. He knows everybody in Hollis. Got it."

When a beef arose with somebody, Jay would be there to keep the peace.

"Not even, 'I'll talk to him,'" remembered Run. "Just, 'It's over. Stop thinking about it.'"

• • •

He was a serviceable mix master in those early days. No Davy "DMX" Reeves or DJ Jazzy Jay. Later, he "became a phenomenal DJ," said Run. Jay did what any smart, aspiring musician would do. He listened to his elders, particularly the more experienced Davy DMX, who adopted his nickname from the drum machine that became hip-hop's Swiss Army knife. Reeves was a multidimensional threat, a seasoned musician who also understood the latest technologies. But it was Jay who became the first star behind the turntables. Jazzy Jeff. Terminator X. They all came later.

And beyond street cred, beyond seriousness in the studio, Jay brought a third, vital element to Run-DMC. He brought them style, the black leather uniform—fedora, chains, and Adidas with no laces and the flap up—that came to define them.

This is another subject that frustrated Run, though it's hard to know exactly why. He didn't like the narrative, the idea that, before Jay, he and Darryl were hopelessly unstylish, a pair of street-scared Urkels. Usually, the argument is made with a pair of snapshots as the key exhibits. The first shows Run and D at the Fever without Jay. Darryl wears a white turtleneck with a chain of some kind and a white sport coat. Run is wearing a black shirt, white pants, and a sport coat of his own with a plaid pattern.

There is also the first promotional photo that Butch Green, later known as Talib Haqq, took of the three. It's 1983 and they're standing against a brick wall. Run could pass as a younger version of Kurtis Blow, with a leather jacket and white jeans. Darryl wears a trench coat over a dress shirt tucked into slacks. He's leaning awkwardly, one hand tucked behind him, and gazing off softly, as if too shy to strike a B-boy pose. Then there's Jay. He's in the center, dark shirt tucked into dark pants, wearing a leather coat, and his hand clutches his thick belt buckle like Dr. J palming a basketball. That isn't just any belt buckle. It spells out his name.

In 1987's *Tougher Than Leather*, Bill Adler's authorized biography of the group, this particular snapshot is held up as prime evidence of their pre-Jay sartorial confusion.

Run, Adler writes, is "maybe halfway there," noting his leather jacket but that "his hair is wrong, an Afro with sideburns, instead of the close-cropped b-boy style." D looks more like a "garden-variety college student than like a rapper."

"I'm going to fix this picture for everybody that laughs at it," Run said later, offering his own critique. "This was a burgundy leather jacket. My brother had a brown one. This was a cool jacket. This was a very cool jacket. And that was some gangster stuff D had on. A trench coat is the flyest thing ever. And I told him to start wearing the glasses. The coolest thing in the entire earth are those glasses. Ever. So it's important that you trust the truth. And this isn't me trying to protect nothing. We wore what everybody else wore.

"Now, Jay," he said, "was the next level of cool."

Style would be an essential part of the cultural revolution sparked by Run-DMC, as essential as the Beatles and their mop tops and collarless suits twenty years earlier.

What they wore—and why they wore it—would not just set them apart. It would work as the sartorial equivalent to their sound—stripped-down, street-savvy, and never meant to be confused with Sugar Hill's disco stable. What Run-DMC wore would usher in the era of brand marketing that eventually made millionaires of 50 Cent, Jay Z, and Dr. Dre. It would also redefine the way black America viewed and expressed itself.

Black intellectuals, looking to assimilate into white-ruled society, sniffed that unlaced sneakers or a sideways cap would set them back, that it spoke to the street thug. Bill Cosby, for one, spent years blasting not just hip-hop but the look of hip-hop. That's why first-generation rappers—Caz, Melle Mel, Kurtis Blow—believed you needed to dress up, play the role, when you got onstage. That you needed a costume, and that costume certainly wouldn't be what you wore on the corner. Caz and the Cold Crush Brothers were probably the hottest MCs on tape in the early '80s. In person, they might as well have been Earth, Wind & Fire, with their white suits, floppy hats (with boas), and disco boots. Blow had started out cool, leather jackets and jeans. By the time Run-DMC emerged, he was wearing shimmering shirts and Jheri curl. Run dismissed the idea that what he, D, and Jay wore was particularly plotted out.

"We wore what every kid would wear," said Run.

• • •

It isn't clear if Jay cared about not being on the group's first three album covers or whether he felt slighted. Fludd doesn't remember any complaints. For one thing, the shows were centered around the DJ.

"First, Jay goes up and starts scratching and he brings DMC out and he brings Run out and the show starts," says Fludd. "Jay and I hung out from a young age and he had no problem getting women, we had no problem getting money. He's trying

Chapter 10
AEROSMITH: REUNITED

The Joe Perry Project played eighty shows in 1982, and 116 in 1983. By now, the Perryless Aerosmith, finally done with *Rock in a Hard Place*, hit the road to support the new record. And even in its diminished state, it was hard to argue on which faction maintained a larger section of the Blue Army.

Bell remembered a trip to Toronto in December, when the Project played the El Mocambo nightclub (capacity: 458) two days before Aerosmith played their gig less than two miles away, at the Maple Leaf Gardens (capacity: 15,728).

"He never said a word about it," said Bell. "If somebody showed up, that was cool, if they didn't, he didn't give a shit. He just wanted to play, and play he did."

There was even a moment, during the set, that they'd be playing "No Substitute for Arrogance" off the second Project record and the band would grind into a longer jam and Perry would throw in the melody of "Dream On" as a counterpoint during his solo.

"It started off as real chaotic and then it would start to ride up, this slow 'Dream On' framework, and it was a statement and it would drive the audiences crazy," said Bell. "What exactly that statement was from night to night, I leave that to the audiences."

The tour dates kept Perry moving, took him around the

country, but the gigs—at such venues as the New England Dragway in Epping, New Hampshire, and Mr. C's Rock Palace in Lowell, Massachusetts—didn't do much to solve the guitarist's financial problems. Collins had to take the next step. He had to get Perry a record deal. Two years had passed since *I've Got the Rock 'n' Rolls Again*, which had peaked at a disappointing number one hundred on the *Billboard* charts before disappearing into the cutout bins. Collins headed to Los Angeles and tried to get meetings. Nobody, he found, was interested in Perry.

One of his biggest targets had been Geffen Records executive John Kalodner. By then, the former music writer had established himself by signing or working with Asia, Foreigner, and Judas Priest. He also was hard to miss in the cocaine-centered music industry.

Kalodner wore white suits and grew his hair long and his beard thick like the bed-in-era Lennon. He didn't do drugs. And he didn't pull punches.

Collins couldn't get a meeting with Kalodner when he headed to Los Angeles, but back in Boston, a call came into the manager's tiny office. Kalodner on line two.

At first, Collins thought it was a joke, and then he heard the voice, the distinctfully nasal tones of negativity. Kalodner had received Perry's latest demo tape.

"Why would you ever let Joe Perry make a piece-of-shit record like this?" Kalodner asked.

"It's nice to meet you," said Collins.

"It's not really nice to meet you," Kalodner said. "What kind of manager are you?"

"He was," Collins said years later, "the first guy in the industry who was honest with me. He told me, the manager's job is to guide him to make great music. You're not doing your job."

That may have been true. What was also true was that Perry had filed for that second mortgage on his house. He would soon lose his collection of guitars, including the prized 1959 Les Paul he had played during Aerosmith's golden era. A sense of desperation hovered over everything.

• • •

Enter Leon Tsilis, national director for artists and repertoire at MCA Records. The label had just been taken over by former Eagles manager Irving Azoff, whose merciless approach—and his height (five-three)—had earned him the nickname "the poisoned dwarf." Azoff had been shedding artists he had inherited and spending big money on new signings, including Joan Jett and Bee Gees singer Barry Gibb.

Tsilis accepted Collins's invitation to Boston to meet Perry and to see the third version of the Joe Perry Project.

"I liked Joe Perry, believe me," said Tsilis. "And I loved Aerosmith. Now, the thing was, they fucked themselves up on drugs. And nobody, no record label, wanted to have something to do with them."

But Collins had good news. Perry, he told Tsilis, was cleaned up, not doing drugs anymore, and Tyler was going through the same program.

"And they're both free agents," said Tsilis. "So my eyes start lighting up."

Was Perry clean? That, ladies and gentlemen of the jury, depends on your definition of "clean."

"Clean to us was not doing heroin, and to be honest, as I look back, it was a bit of a con, but not meant to be," said Collins. "We kind of conned ourselves. I wasn't a heroin addict, and you've got to remember, when I met Joe, I was a drinker. I was an Irish kid from Waltham who loved to drink, and I didn't do cocaine until right around that time, and I never did opiates. So I thought that was clean."

Collins left nothing to chance. Perry wasn't just off drugs. He was on a health kick and working out at the gym. Longtime Aerosmith photographer Ron Pownall was brought in to snap shots of Perry pumping iron. Never mind that in the photos, the shirtless Perry is wearing jeans and a watch. Or that another picture—not released then, but put in Perry's autobiography years later—shows the guitarist at a recording session with his trusty bottle of Jack Daniel's next to him. Pownall's photos were just the start.

What came next was a visit as choreographed as *Swan Lake*.

It started as soon as Tsilis got off the plane at Logan Airport.

Collins knew he could call on Mark Parenteau, the popular afternoon DJ on the only radio station that mattered, WBCN-FM, 104.1. "The Rock of Boston" was one of the country's most influential stations, with programmers everywhere following its lead. WBCN was also intensely local. Peter Wolf, billing himself as the Woofa Goofa, did the overnight shift at the station in the late 1960s before breaking out as the lead singer of the J. Geils Band. And the station had done a live broadcast of Aerosmith's 1973 gig at Paul's Mall. Parenteau was particularly tight with Collins and Perry. They did drugs together, crashed at one another's places. And now, Collins enlisted Parenteau to help Perry get a record deal.

When Collins picked Tsilis up at the airport, his assistant called Parenteau. By the time they got the record exec's luggage and hopped in the limo, the plan had kicked into play. The driver flipped on the radio and, lucky them, it was "Joe Perry Day" on WBCN.

Boston has always been a small town, a provincial city where "everybody knows your name," as the chorus went in the theme to the popular 1980s sitcom *Cheers*. Tsilis remembers a dinner at the Bull & Finch, the restaurant whose facade served as the setup shot for the TV show. He remembers Perry didn't even take a drink. Collins made sure to have an endless stream of admirers stopping at the table, interrupting to let Perry know how much they were looking forward to his next record.

If Perry was using, he didn't show it.

"He didn't do anything," Tsilis said. "He was very coherent."

By the next morning, they began talking about the deal. Perry wasn't going to break the bank. MCA signed him for just $75,000. He viewed it as a great deal, just a fraction of the multimillion-dollar contract the label would give Joan Jett.

• • •

"But Joe wasn't going to get more than that," said Tsilis. "They were taking a chance. They were taking a shot. They figured if it did happen and Aerosmith got back together, they might have a shot with a reformed Aerosmith."

By now, Ronnie Stewart had seen enough. He quit early in the sessions and was replaced by drummer Joe Pet.

For the first two solo records, Perry had been able to lean on veteran producers Jack Douglas and Bruce Botnick. This time, he produced on his own. There would be an almost stubborn, stripped-down approach. This was 1983. Eddie Van Halen's explorations with his Oberheim keyboard would lead to his band's most successful single, "Jump." Perry would issue a proud promise, in bold and italicized letterhead on the back cover of the album that became *Once a Rocker, Always a Rocker*: "There are no synthesizers on this album."

The creative well wasn't exactly overflowing. Tsilis gave Perry a song, "Women in Chains," from a group of writers in Nashville. There would be an unexceptional cover of glam icon Marc Bolan's "Bang a Gong." The other seven songs were credited to Perry and Bell.

Years later, Tsilis said he still liked the record a lot. He is in rare company. While "Let the Music Do the Talking" would eventually be rerecorded by Aerosmith and remain a part of the band's live shows, none of the ten songs on *Rocker* found their way out of 1983. In reality, the only stroke of luck for Perry connected to the third Project record came during the video shoot for "Black Velvet Pants." That's where he met Billie Montgomery, a model enlisted for the video to walk to the concert venue, hop onstage, and, awkwardly and in heels, grab a saxophone and simulate joining the band.

Montgomery and Perry were drawn to each other, which created high drama during the dysfunction of those years. Newly divorced, he had been seeing Glenda McNeil, who was the band's hairdresser. (Note Bell's monster perm and Perry's feathered locks on *Rocker's* album cover.) McNeil didn't take kindly to the young model moving in. During the video shoot, she started a fistfight with Montgomery.

That was the only excitement that seemed to surround *Once a Rocker, Always a Rocker.* The record—on which Parenteau was credited with playing "chains" on one song—sold forty thousand copies after its release in September 1983.

The Toxic Twins were no longer rock and roll bad boys. They were crashing on couches or staying in hotels. Krebs and Leber, their managers, were withholding money from them, trying to keep them from spending it all on drugs. They kept their things in cardboard boxes wrapped in twine. The cars were gone, the girls were gone, the future seemed bleak. That's when they decided to start talking again.

• • •

It didn't go well at first.

At a gig in Worcester, just before Thanksgiving 1982, Perry showed up, and he and Tyler holed up in the dressing room.

"They went back into the one thing they could agree on," said Whitford. "Get high."

When the band took the stage, Whitford and Perry stood in back, watching them play. Watching Tyler collapse.

"And everybody, of course, blamed Joe," said Whitford. "It had to be Joe. He brought drugs. And years later, when the truth finally came out, Joe did not bring the drugs. Steven had the drugs."

A lot of people take credit for bringing them back together. Collins for helping the group get out of their deal with Leber and Krebs and Columbia. Tyler for reaching out to Perry when he heard he was considering joining Alice Cooper's band. Finally, there's Rick Dufay.

"The band I was in toward the end was terrible," he said. "Business was bad. The relationship with the manager was bad. Everyone was getting way too high."

In late October 1983, Dufay told Tyler they were going to go see Perry at the Bottom Line in New York City, where the Project was playing. Backstage after the show, he sat them both down.

"Joe, the band, even with me, it sucks," he said. "And the band we just saw, it sucked. You guys got to talk."

He walked out and told the security guard not to let them out for a half hour.

Years later, when Aerosmith was being inducted into the Rock and Roll Hall of Fame, Perry singled out Dufay for "committing career suicide." Dufay laughed when he heard that.

"Career suicide?" he said. "You got to be fucking kidding me. I was saving my life getting out of that."

Chapter 11

RUN-DMC: DOWN WITH KING KURT

Kurtis Blow wasn't happy. He had been there first, rising with "The Breaks," the first rap song to be certified gold when it came out in 1980. He worked the circuit hard over the next five years, whether his new records sold or, as was often the case, barely cracked the Top 200. And even during that dry spell, Blow made his mark. The Clash had him open for them at Pier 84 when they came to New York City in 1982. He also helped in the studio, getting credit for mixing Run-DMC's debut single, "It's Like That," and producing the first two Fat Boys records. Finally, in 1985, Blow landed back on the charts with "If I Ruled the World," a song off his sixth album, *America*.

But by then, something had shifted. Even if his sound had never been hard-core, at least Blow had looked the part. Now the wiry kid with the bare chest and the "Am I really here?" half smile looked like he could be busting a move with Billy Ocean, all Jheri curl, glittery shirts, and backup girls. Run-DMC would be the ones getting props for their street look, taking the stage in black leather, Kangols, and unlaced Adidas. This image reversal still bothers Blow. Forget the look. Didn't anybody know where they were from? He was the scrapper from the street. Run-DMC were the softies.

"That was all marketing and image," said Blow. "The actual reality of the whole matter is I was a street kid from Harlem and they were from suburbia and had parents and lived in a house. And they're from Queens."

It became, like everything else Russell Simmons touched, a battle for not just sales but reputation. Kurt's standing as his original client, a pioneer, didn't mean much now. Blow had staked his claim to his title as the original King of Rap, a designation referenced in print by no less than the *New York Times*. Then DMC came along, the "devastating mic controller," and declared that he was not only the king of rap, he was something more. "I'm the King of Rock," he boomed on the title track of Run-DMC's second album, released two weeks into 1985. "Sucker M.C.'s can call me sire."

If Kurt had a problem with that, he could always talk to Run-DMC's manager, Russell, who was also both his own manager and his protégé's older brother.

"I hated it, I hated it," Blow said of the competition. "I loved those guys, but competition, there was a thing when you're successful, when you're on the mountaintop, the whole thing is to get you off of that mountaintop. When Run saw that Kurtis Blow was coming, we were thrust into this competitive mode, which really destroyed our relationship."

DMC, who had never had a close relationship with Blow—Kurt was Run's and Russell's guy—didn't feel as if he had wronged anyone.

"Kurt really wasn't nice to me after I started saying I was the king," said DMC. "He was the king. That was his moniker. The shit was 'Who the fuck are these motherfuckers from soft-ass Queens?'"

The public's first hint of Blow's discontent came during the summer of 1985 when he walked away from the wildly successful Fresh Fest tour, a package road show that featured the Fat Boys, Whodini, Run-DMC, and Blow.

"Mr. Blow Won't Show but 'Fresh Fest' Goes On," read the headline in the *Chicago Sun-Times*.

"The last show we did before heading for Chicago, I was going on next to last, the spot for the star, and they changed it," Blow complained to the paper. "Everyone said, 'It's cool, it's cool, we'll change it back' but they didn't. For that reason, the 'Blow' is no show."

What's worse, he said, the Fat Boys were put in his star spot.

"I made the Fat Boys," he told the *Sun-Times*. "Whodini. The Fat Boys. Run-DMC . . . I made those groups. Oh yeah, they claim to be my friends, they say they love me so much, but when it came down to it, boom! They really laid it on me."

In the article, Blow did make a promise to his fans. That fall, Warner Bros. would release the film *Krush Groove,* meant to tell the story of the birth of Def Jam Records with some creative license. He would be playing the King of Rap, or, as he put it, "I'm playing myself."

• • •

Krush Groove arrived amid a slew of rap-inspired films, including a genuine box office smash (*Breakin'*) and a bust of a film (*Body Rock*) that starred soap opera hottie Lorenzo Lamas as a rapper turned break-dancer named Chilly D.

Krush Groove is, in every way, the cinematic embodiment of the turmoil inside the Run-DMC/Rush Productions/Def Jam family. Director Michael Schultz came to the table with a solid record, having made the adolescent drama *Cooley High* and the musical comedy *Car Wash*. (He had also directed 1978's big-budget bust *Sgt. Pepper's Lonely Hearts Club Band*, but most blamed producer Robert Stigwood, Peter Frampton, and the Bee Gees for that disaster.)

The producers made their first mistake in the casting. They signed on baby-faced Blair Underwood, just twenty and unknown, to play Russell Simmons, who, in real life, had a decided edge and deliciously profane sense of humor. (Blow, Run-DMC, the Fat Boys, and Rick Rubin played themselves.) Sheila E., the percussionist and Prince protégé, was thrust into a starring role, even though she couldn't act and was a pop singer with no connection to hip-hop. Then they saddled E. with a fake romantic storyline with the Simmons character, Russell Walker, meant to add a tense rivalry between the brothers. All of it came off as remarkably phony, not least because of Run's unconvincing acting job. The *Krush Groove* team also made another noticeable decision, this one of omission.

Larry Smith had served as the musical supervisor of *Rappin'*, the weak attempt to add a third film to the *Breakin'* franchise. But in *Krush Groove*, he was MIA. True, he wasn't part of Def Jam, but neither were Run-DMC, the Fat Boys, or Sheila E.

Smith's absence is accentuated in the opening scene, as Run-DMC lay down "King of Rock" with Rubin behind the board. That's a Smith production and one that Rubin, in real life, didn't particularly like. It's also bizarre that Smith is never mentioned in *Krush Groove*, when the movie's title is taken from the beat that he and Simmons created.

The soundtrack adds to the disharmony. There are ten songs and nine different producers—tracks done by the prefame Beastie Boys and LL Cool J alongside Sheila E., the Gap Band, and Debbie Harry. The most telling moment comes on the final song, "Krush Groovin'," meant to be a collaboration between Sheila E., Blow, the Fat Boys, and Run-DMC.

Rubin, now overseeing Run-DMC, despised the soft R&B groove that Blow centered the track around. So he simply ignored the song produced by Simmons and Blow and recorded a completely independent, forty-eight-second section that he surgically inserted after the Fat Boys rapped. The smooth, jazzy guitar line, the bass, and keyboards give way to a raw, banging middle section.

"Rick said, 'I cannot take it,'" said Simmons. "He went into the studio by himself, and he and Run-DMC cut in a new part, and it sounds great. It sounds explosive and new."

Blow at first fought the change.

"Because, here's another producer and I'm producing the soundtrack and 'What do you mean you're going to bring in another producer and cut a whole new track to the track I just loved?' But then I heard the sound. The actual beat. I couldn't deny it. There was nothing I could say. It was so dope, so fresh. As a matter of fact, I had to redo my part that came after their part."

The final battle between Blow and Run-DMC, as Darryl remembered it, took place the next spring at the New York Music Awards.

In the dressing room at Madison Square Garden, Blow waited until he was alone with DMC and then approached. By now, it had been more than a year since *King of Rock* had come out, an album that had spent fifty-six weeks on the *Billboard* charts and made Run-DMC rap's first superstars. They were the only hip-hop group to perform at the massive Live Aid festival, doing a short set between Black Sabbath and REO Speedwagon at a packed JFK Stadium in Philadelphia. *Raising Hell* would arrive within months.

"You, DMC, you got to stop saying you're the king," Darryl remembered Blow hollering at him.

Run got backstage a few minutes later and could tell something was wrong.

"D, what's happening?" he asked.

"Kurt said I isn't no king anymore," said DMC.

DMC watched Run chase Blow down in the middle of Felt Forum, curse him out, and let him know that they can say they're kings, queens, whatever the fuck they want to be. This was no small thing.

"Because Run was the Son of Kurtis Blow," DMC said. "That's the day the father had to let the son go."

• • •

Another relationship was also ending, though with less drama. For Larry Smith, the producer who had taken them from his Cadillac to Live Aid, *King of Rock* would mark the end of his time with Run-DMC. It was, to say the least, a curious exit. Here was the most successful rap producer of his time splitting with the group he had nurtured, developed, and grown into arena stars. And what's more, nobody seemed to acknowledge that a split was actually taking place. It went unreported in the press, which seemed already mesmerized by Simmons and

Hip-hop pioneers, as children

Jason "Jam Master Jay" Mizell at the turntables

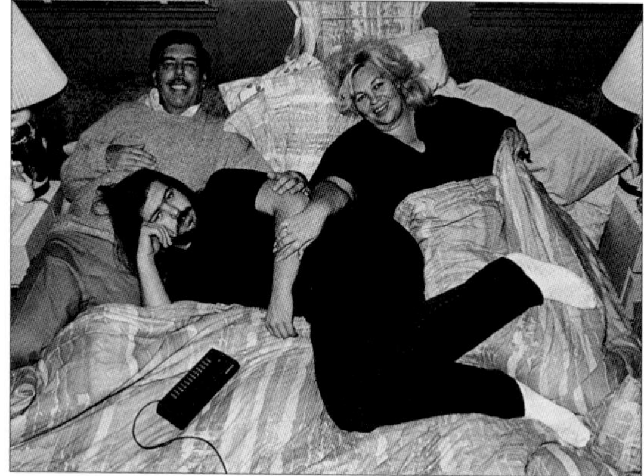

The Rubins. Mickey, a shoe wholesaler, Linda, a housewife, and Rick, the only son

Rick Rubin, the "king" of rap

Debbie Harry (ctr) and Blondie filming their "Rapture" video. Fab 5 Freddy in the background.

DJ Lovebug, Busy Bee, and Grandmaster Caz at the Celebrity Club, 1980

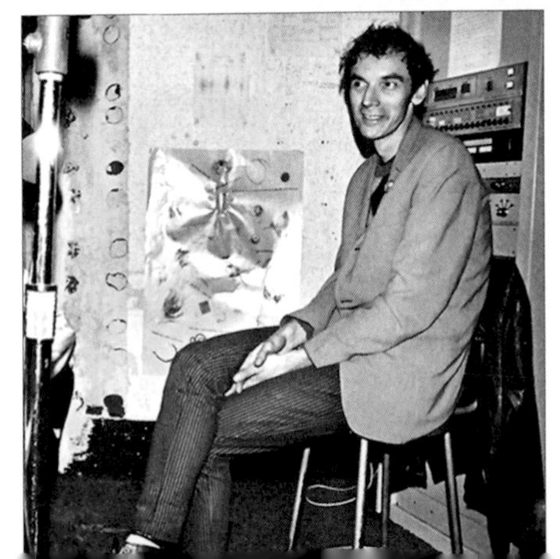

Ed Bahlman, founder of 99 Records and one of Rubin's earliest mentors

Run-DMC's first publicity photo

Bobby Gas, Davy DMX, Kurtis Blow, and Larry Smith on bass

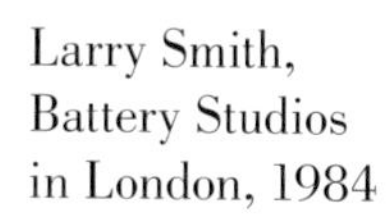

Larry Smith, Battery Studios in London, 1984

Joe Perry Project, Cowboy Mach edition

Rick Rubin runs into Run in NYC, 1987

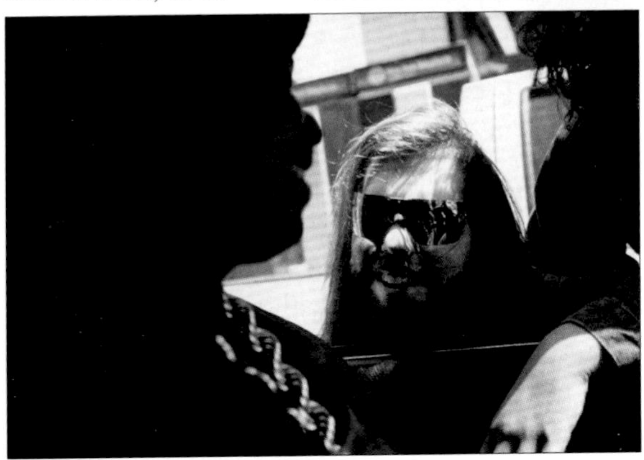

BELOW: Run-DMC, Beastie Boys on the bus. Together Forever Tour, 1987.

Steven Tyler and his bongos. 1981

Aerosmith, arena stars, 1978

RIGHT: Joe Perry, Meadowlands in New Jersey, August 6, 1978

A "fresh" start. Aerosmith with Jimmy Crespo. Cumberland Civic Center in Portland, Maine, December 6, 1979.

Tim Collins with his new client, October 5, 1983

Joe Perry "working out" at a Boston health club, October 5, 1983.

Cleveland Stadium, July 28, 1979. After this show, Perry would quit backstage.

Rick Rubin, Room 402, fall 1981

Rick Rubin, holding record, with a friend at the famous Weinstein dorm bikini contest party, 1984.

Steven Tyler and Jimmy Crespo, 1983

Not clean but back together, 1984.

Run-DMC, Russell Simmons with Profile co-founders Steve Plotnicki and Cory Robbins

Just before they recorded, photographer Danny Sanchez pulled them into the hallway for a portrait for *Spin* magazine.

eager to embrace Rubin. But Run and D also admit that they never really asked why Smith was gone.

"Did I whine about no Larry?" said Run. "Remember, there's no need to whine. I don't know what Russell's dealing with."

As far as Bill Adler's concerned, there is a clear moment when the split occurred: August 3, 1985. That's when Run-DMC went out to Los Angeles to appear on Dick Clark's *American Bandstand*. They performed "King of Rock," the hit at the time, but then they performed a version of "Jam Master Jammin'" that was different from the one produced by Smith for their second album. This one featured a mix from Rick Rubin, who played barre chords. Rubin also went out to L.A. Smith didn't.

The operative excuse or justification became Whodini, Smith's other big success. Because the platinum-selling group were signed to the London-based Jive Records, recording their follow-up to 1984's *Escape* had to take place overseas. Smith, the story went, simply couldn't produce on both sides of the ocean at the same time.

"Run-DMC was a platinum group. Whodini was a platinum group," said Russell Simmons. "And then, Rick comes along and he's helping to do Run-DMC. We're all busy. We're high, we're making records. I don't think he felt put off by Run-DMC at the time."

Cey Adams, Def Jam's creative director in the 1980s, saw the shift from Smith to Rubin as very natural, driven more by the nature of the central figures than any sort of ruthless desire to push anybody out.

"Rick had a vision of where he wanted to see the music go," Adams said. "I hate to say it, but I don't know that Larry was a dreamer in that way. Larry was excited about making music, and he might have been content. Nobody at that time could have imagined becoming a superproducer. If Larry was a good producer, having aspirations to be a great producer, what did it look like before that? Quincy Jones was maybe the only guy. Maybe Nile Rodgers and Bernard Edwards. I don't know that Larry saw what the future looked like. Rick had an idea of wanting something very specific for himself as an individual. He was not going to fail. He was going to win, win, win and keep winning, and I think sadly this is sort of the difference between coming from Hollis, Queens, and wanting to be a producer and being somebody who wants to be one of the greatest producers that anybody has ever seen."

Did Smith even care about what went down?

At first, he probably had no idea of what had shifted. Sal Abbatiello believed it would have been totally out of character for Smith to get jealous of Rubin and Simmons for partnering to create Def Jam. He never talked about wanting to be a record mogul. He just wanted to play.

"And all he cared about was being with his boys and being high and making music," said Abbatiello. "He lived at the Fever. That was his place. He had a little Puerto Rican friend named Trini who was his coke dealer. I don't even remember any press on Larry back in the day. No one would know he made those records."

Smith never said much publicly about what happened. In an interview in *Blues & Soul* in late 1985, he merely referenced a split with Simmons "through contract problems with Profile."

The closest he came to grousing was in a *Billboard* piece written by Nelson George in 1987.

"I went up to talk to some executives about producing rap artists, and they began telling me about Rick Rubin from uptown says this or that—that Rubin is the king of rap," Smith said. "I didn't find that funny. Rick is a downtown kid from New York University. What about Jimmy Spicer and Melle Mel and the other real uptown kids who live this music? Sometimes this business is wild."

When he was working with Whodini in London in 1985, there was some grumbling, but nothing dramatic.

"Those were his boys," said Whodini's Jalil Hutchins. "Larry loved Run-DMC. Just like he loved us. He just said, 'The boys cut me off. Let's do our thing.'"

Michelle Charters, who married Smith in 1986, believes he hid his pain about the split.

"What happened between Russell and Larry was very personal, even though Russell would say, 'No, it's the business,' and Larry, in front of people, would say, 'It's what you have to do.' Behind closed doors, in our home, in our room, it wasn't the case. It was heartbreaking, and it hurt him."

• • •

Smith's decline was precipitous. Whodini's *Open Sesame* went gold, not platinum, when it came out in 1987. Smith's attempt to work with Grandmaster Flash and the Furious Five during their reunion led to just one song, "Gold," and the song flopped.

Hip-hop was changing, with thicker productions—stacked

with samples—driving Public Enemy, the Beastie Boys, and Eric B. & Rakim. Marley Marl, Dre, and Hank Shocklee and the Bomb Squad pushed the rhythmic boundaries.

"I think he may have felt out of place as many of the guys from that early era of hip-hop production," said Bill Stephney, the former Public Enemy producer who went on to become president of Def Jam Recordings in the late 1980s. "The musician DJ could do that sort of funk that led into hip-hop. Once sampling took over, it was kind of like the horse-drawn carriage being replaced by the Model T."

"We had a phone in our house that had four individual lines coming through to it," Michelle Charters remembered. "The top line was the personal family line. If any of the other three lines rung, we knew it was business. The only way I can say it, at times I felt like I was working for AT&T, because the three lines would go on crazy for Larry to lay down tracks, to go meet somebody. There were two things he kept getting asked, but he hated. One was 'I want you to make this group sound like Run-DMC and Whodini.' Larry would say no. 'I can make your guy sound the best that he can be, but I'm not going to make him sound like Whodini,' and he wouldn't. The other thing he would not do was sample. So when he kept refusing to sample stuff, the calls started diminishing. Soon, no one called."

Drugs also began to take over. Smith had always been a user. Everybody had.

"You can't be sober in a room full of people getting high," said Danny Simmons. "It wasn't an aberration like, 'Oh, that guy's over there getting high.' You would be an aberration if you weren't being high. But what started to happen is that it started interfering with how people lived and they would say, 'This is not working, this ain't going to work with what's happening in my life.'"

Danny Simmons cleaned up. So did Russell. But Larry Smith got into crack. He lost Charters, who moved back home to England. Then he lost his house.

"It got so bad," Russell Simmons remembered, "he was out, living in his car, he had a girlfriend, this little crack girl, and he had his girlfriend selling pussy."

The last time Danny Simmons saw Smith was in the late '80s at a big barbecue he was hosting. By then, Danny had cleaned up and had been working as a drug counselor. Fred Buggs, Smith's childhood friend, begged Danny for help. Smith went into the bathroom to smoke crack and wouldn't come out.

• • •

In 2004, Spyder-D interviewed Smith over the phone for his website. Spyder-D was not an impartial witness. He always found the transfer of production power, from Smith to Rubin, more than unsettling. He looked at Simmons, Rubin, and Lyor Cohen, the triumvirate of industry moguls, and felt that it should have been a group of four.

"Rick became who he became because he rolled with Russell," said Spyder. "Lyor Cohen went from road manager to number two man on the totem pole at Warner. Are you kidding me? That doesn't happen without Russell Simmons. He made those men. That should have been Larry. Without Larry doing what he did, Run-DMC doesn't blow up like they do. Russell Simmons does not blow up like he does. If Run-DMC is a flop,

Russell Simmons never meets a Lyor Cohen. Def Jam is never associated with CBS. If you remove Larry Smith from any of that equation, arguably hip-hop is not where it is right now."

During that phone interview, Spyder admitted he pushed Smith to complain about Simmons, Rubin, and the way he fell out of favor. Smith wouldn't.

"Russell," he said at one point, "was the businessman of our situation at that time. All I cared about was making music."

And when Spyder declared that he hated the fact that Simmons and Smith parted, Smith again demurred.

Rubin was just different. He embraced the high theater of the entertainment industry, and when he needed to—for a Def Jam promo clip, an interview with a reporter, a meeting with the record company bigwigs—he could effortlessly slip into his thuggish World Wrestling Federation persona. He wanted to make videos, then movies, then a revolution. Larry Smith wanted to chill with his guys, hang in the studio, play music.

For Russell to become what he became, Larry told Spyder that day, "he had to leave me behind."

Part Two

1986

Chapter 12
CREATING RICK RUBIN

Trashy or cool or ironic or just plain undecipherable. The beauty of those days and that place was how you could really be anyone. Like the cartoon grapplers on *WWF Championship Wrestling*, you could adopt whatever persona the moment called for. Gather around Robin Byrd's nasty soft-porn cable show or discuss the merits of French filmmaker Jean-Pierre Melville. Bikini contests, prank calls, record label meetings in your dorm room, all of them sloshing around in the greatest cocktail party of your mind.

"There was a security guard, but we had kegs at our parties," remembered Denise Capuozzo, who arrived at NYU's Weinstein Hall in the fall of 1983. "The drinking age had just gone to twenty-one, but nobody seemed to care. People were throwing statues off the roof. It kind of felt like the inmates were running the asylum."

Weinstein became famous, mainly for the students who moved through it in the 1980s, including actor Philip Seymour Hoffman, future MTV VJ Martha Quinn, and future New York mayor Bill de Blasio. But nobody embodied the spirit of the dorm more than a coddled Jewish kid from Lido Beach who had once had dreams of being a professional magician.

By the time Rick Rubin got to Weinstein, in the fall of 1981, music wasn't just a radio station in the background during study sessions. It was at the center of his life. Rubin had massive Cerwin-Vega speakers that boomed through the dorm walls. Some called him Rick Rock. Some used other names.

"When he first moved in, I thought, 'This guy's a jerk,'" remembered Bob Giordano, who was entering his senior year when he met Rubin. "I was way more Catholic in those days, and I was afraid of people who were a little weird or something. But the greatest thing I found out is that sometimes people you think are going to be jerks end up being the best people. Because they have nothing to hide."

Mike Espindle, who had come to NYU as a premed student but ended up majoring in journalism, remembered a friend bringing Rubin to his room. He had a nice Gibson guitar and he liked to play power chords loud. Later, Espindle would become the lead singer—or screamer—in Rubin's punk rock band, Hose.

"He had already been in a band called the Pricks in Long Island that had played in the city," said Espindle. "And when I met him he had three very cool things he had done. He had been in the Pricks. I think he worked for some of the wrestling magazines doing photography. Really before wrestling broke out. And he had some relationship with the Plasmatics. I don't remember what it was exactly. Those were the things that sort of impressed me."

The beard came later. The sunglasses, too.

"We went and saw the Dirty Harry movie *Sudden Impact*," said Espindle. "Harry's wearing a specific kind of sunglasses.

Rick went out and got those when it happened. He was developing the persona that we know."

In the world of hip-hop, where outsiders could be booed offstage for living two blocks outside the neighborhood, Rubin seemed utterly unconcerned about street cred. He did nothing to hide that he had grown up in comfort in suburbia.

He was an only child. Mickey worked as a shoe wholesaler. Linda stayed home. They always supported Ricky. As a boy, he had become obsessed with magic. In high school, he'd been encouraged by a teacher to play music and his parents bought him a Gibson.

When Espindle visited the house, he saw that Rubin had done up his room to resemble the Danceteria. There was stage seating along the walls, club-style bleachers.

"You know, you went over there and Mickey would make you matzo brie and Linda would pour love all over Rick," said Espindle. "The one thing his parents did that others didn't is that he was just very secure in that upbringing."

Even after he started getting a name, when no less than the *Village Voice* slapped him on the cover and declared him "The King of Rap," Rubin never tried to hide Lido Beach. When the *Voice* wanted to photograph him, he didn't force Jim Harrison to catch him at the Fever during a late-night jam or cruising down Broadway in a lowrider. He invited him to meet the parents. The images Harrison captured are stunningly unpretentious. There he lay, the "King" in tube socks and black jeans, splayed on his side across his parents' bed. Mickey has his hand resting on his son's elbow. Linda, under the covers, puts her right hand on his wrist. That position, a reflex not a pose, tells you everything you need to know. This was a special boy.

Mickey even boasts, in that same cover story, that Rick used to sleep between them until after his twelfth birthday.

"He thought a green boogie man lived in the closet," Linda said.

"When he comes home without a girl," Mickey confided, "sometimes he still sleeps with us."

Rick Rubin had arrived at Weinstein without a whisker, a freshman surrounded by books and papers. But he was already impossible to miss.

"In the middle of the night, you would see him walking across the lobby getting some food, and he would be wearing a wool hat, sunglasses, and leg warmers," said Tim Sommer, a fellow NYU student and a radio DJ who would play an important role in pushing rap at MTV. "We always thought he was a weird figure, but when you began talking to him, you saw he had this encyclopedic knowledge of music and film."

By the fall of 1982, Rubin had transformed his surroundings. That September, Adam Dubin arrived at Weinstein, ready to move in and start his freshman year. An older kid met him and helped load everything onto a cart. They rolled down the hallway, the upperclassman looking back.

Room 712?

"Your roommate is some kind of musician or something," the older kid said with a shrug.

He did not sound impressed.

At the door, Dubin paused. He can regenerate that mental snapshot even decades later.

The shades were drawn. The room was completely dark, except for one light, which was muted by a red do-rag draped over it. The desks were in the center of the room, pushed together and covered by two turntables, a mixer, and a tangle of wires. The dressers and every other surface in the room were covered with boxes of records and speakers. Sitting on the bed was a pudgy kid all in black. He wore sunglasses.

Dubin looked around.

"Where are you supposed to do homework?"

"Homework is to be done in the library," the older kid said in a thick Long Island baritone that may have been a put-on.

Okay. They got to talking. Rubin studied film. That was also Dubin's plan. A wave of relief washed over the freshman. They would have something in common, particularly that neither of them would be getting up at seven a.m. for a civil engineering class.

Dubin asked about the turntables. He had never seen that kind of rig. Rubin told him that he DJ'd a lot and then asked Dubin what bands he liked.

"I don't know," Dubin stumbled. "The Rolling Stones?"

Rubin looked down. "Ugh." Before long, Rubin began to offer the younger kid his version of a musical education. He picked through his vinyl, sharing the hard rock and punk, including AC/DC, Aerosmith, and Motörhead. Then Rubin got into the hip-hop records. Kurtis Blow, the Sugar Hill Gang, and, his favorite, the Treacherous Three. Rubin explained why he had two copies of AC/DC's *Back in Black*. To mix the beat. He also showed him a record of his sloppy slash band, Hose.

Rubin loved hardcore, especially Flipper, the punk rock pranksters whose sludgy, bass-heavy music would influence everyone from Jane's Addiction to Nirvana. He had arrived at NYU with the Pricks, a group he proudly let everyone know had played Max's Kansas City and been thrown out for breaking furniture, remembered Giordano.

But even as he continued with Hose, Rubin seemed to be moving on from punk. He could see a hardcore ceiling, a limit to that music's reach. Hip-hop was where he saw the future. It was, as his friend and later producing partner George Drakoulias described it, "black punk rock."

"I think the difference is that there was a closed-mindedness in the white community toward punk," Rubin said, looking back. "Punk was a very niche thing, and hip-hop started as a very niche thing, but it was able to grow. It's got possibilities, not commercial possibilities, but momentum possibilities. A feeling of seeing something you love shared and having more people to talk about it with was exciting. The punk rock world was a small world and getting smaller. And the hip-hop world was a small world growing and getting bigger, and that felt good. It felt like an energetic pull."

There was one thing that bugged him about hip-hop, and it was no small thing. Rubin would go to a live gig and be blown away by the energy. Then he would hear those same groups on record and they'd be soft, flattened by the production. Call it the curse of "Rapper's Delight."

What made those records so dull wasn't that the early rap

producers were amateurs. It was that they were actually too professional. They understood how to work in a studio, they knew what a hit record was supposed to sound like. A hit record should be slick, radio-friendly, produced.

"When they applied that experience to what they thought rap music was supposed to sound like, they missed the point," Rubin said. "Because that's not what it was supposed to sound like. To us, anyway. We thought very much of a DJ culture, sample-oriented, drum machine–based music, and that's what it would sound like if you went to a club. You would hear drum machines. You would hear breaks from rock records and funk records. And MC'ing over that. That was the most exciting energy."

This problem wasn't exclusive to hip-hop. And in a way, it became the guiding principle that would make Rubin the greatest record producer of his time. He didn't worry about the sound of the moment or chasing what the older and more conservative record and radio executives thought might maintain their fiefdoms. He cared about the sound in his head. This extended beyond hip-hop. It's also how he stripped down the music of Johnny Cash and Neil Diamond to help them revive their careers. That vision governed everything, whether Rubin was working with metal heads Slayer, hard-core rappers the Geto Boys, or the Dixie Chicks.

As a music lover first, Rubin cared deeply about getting the sound right. It *still* bothers Rubin that nobody could capture his favorite go-go band on vinyl.

"If you listen to Trouble Funk live, it was the most incredible thing," said Rubin. "If you hear the album they made after they got signed to Island Records, it's like everything that was great about Trouble Funk got taken away."

So much early rap, the stuff on Sugar Hill, Tuff City, everything reminded him of Evelyn "Champagne" King, best known for her 1978 disco hit "Shame."

"But instead of having Evelyn 'Champagne' King sing on it, they would have someone rap on it, and they would think that it was the same," Rubin said. "Because they didn't understand."

He understood. He just had to figure out how to get that sound onto a record and then get that record to the world.

• • •

There would be two mentors, each of them invaluable.

One would be a kind of philosophical guru, a guide for understanding how to nurture and understand the creative process and maintain artistic integrity.

The other would be more nuts-and-bolts, the one who would teach him how to take his art and turn it into a salable product. A record.

Ric Menello and Ed Bahlman also, without intending to, showed Rubin something else. The limits of misfitdom. You could be brilliant, iconoclastic, uncompromising, but if you could not function in mainstream society, you'd eventually disappear.

Start with Menello. He was the first guy anybody entering Weinstein would meet. He ran the front desk. Menello seemed much older than his years, what with his beard, bald pate, and extra pounds. But he was only in his early thirties when he and Rubin met. Menello had graduated in 1974 from Washington

Square College, a branch of NYU created for commuter students, before settling in at the overnight shift.

Crazy in a good way, is how he would often be described.

"He had the best, cackling voice, a real maniacal kind of like—*heh heh heh*—giggle to him," said Gretchen Viehmann, who arrived at NYU in 1983. "Not only did he know everything, but Mr. Ric went kind of beyond that."

"The day kind of moved toward midnight, and at midnight this great thing happened," said Dubin. "Menello took over the front desk, and at Menello's front desk, we all learned how films were made and why films were good. He was like an Orson Welles–type character."

"He loved movies," said Giordano. "He was short and fat and you could irritate him very easily and he would yell and scream at you. I loved the guy and learned so much from him, but he was kind of like a big baby because he was an only child. But he was an invaluable resource for us."

Students would come downstairs to pick up mail, leave notes, or use a pay phone. Menello, at his perch, was less a security guard than an intellectual gatekeeper. The TV would be on at all hours, with black-and-white films and Mary Tyler Moore, Bob Newhart, and always Abbott and Costello. They debated art, music, ordered take-out Chinese or from Sarge's Deli, if they really wanted to splurge.

During the day, Rubin might go to one of William K. Everson's film classes. They'd talk Hitchcock or horror films. Everson showed *Curse of the Demon* and *Targets*, the latter an early Bogdanovich classic that's more suspense than gore. There was also *Seconds*, the John Frankenheimer mystery starring Rock Hudson.

"Everson was terrific in that he was profound and erudite," remembered Dubin. "When we would see these things, we would come back to the front desk and Menello would kind of give us the full background."

Make no mistake. Menello wasn't just an oddball. He had a stunning knowledge of film history. Later, he and Dubin would codirect the classic Beastie Boys video for "(You Gotta) Fight for Your Right (To Party!)," presenting the asshole rap classic as a clear homage to Blake Edwards's *Breakfast at Tiffany's*. He directed the stunning black-and-white video for LL Cool J's "Going Back to Cali." Even after Rubin got famous and moved out to California, he would keep Menello in circulation. It did not matter that the mentor was increasingly a victim of his own eccentricities, his apartment littered with food containers and books. Menello took calls from friends of Rubin looking to bounce film ideas off him.

Director James Gray picked Menello's brain, and he and Rubin began paying his rent. Menello received a writing credit on two of Gray's films, 2008's *Two Lovers* and 2013's *The Immigrant*. That same year, director Wes Anderson, another Rubin friend, contributed to an appreciation written in the *New Yorker* after Menello's death at just sixty.

"He knew every movie, I can tell you that," Anderson offered. "He was the only person I've met who you just couldn't stump and so you didn't try—he was instead a resource and was very overtly thought of that way by a large circle."

Rubin, whose NYU degree would be in film and television,

drew on Menello's photographic memory and encyclopedic knowledge of movie history.

"I probably learned more from him than I did in film school," he said.

• • •

Ed Bahlman, Rubin's other mentor, was everything Menello was not. Mysterious. Quiet. Awkward. Almost unhealthily thin.

"He looked a bit like a heron," said Vivien Goldman, the British-born writer and musician who met Bahlman in 1980 while searching for somebody to put out a record.

She had heard the guy who ran the shop at 99 MacDougal Street didn't just sell music, he put it out on his small label. She headed to the Village and played Bahlman "Launderette," a dub pop song she had recorded with the help of P.I.L. front man and former Sex Pistol John Lydon.

"He had something of the sort of, almost an academic vibe or being very intense, intelligent, inward," she said. "Ed, I perceived him as more of a retiring type. An introvert. One sensed he was quite a complicated person. I don't think I really socialized with him. I felt he was an honest, honorable type. As to whether I got any money, I don't really think I did. I think he gave me some money, he gave me an advance. I'm guessing it was a couple of hundred. Maybe five hundred dollars. Some sum. It wasn't completely nothing."

As a boy, Ed Bahlman certainly did not seem destined to work in a record store, never mind start an influential label.

He grew up in Brooklyn, sharing a room with his younger brother, Bill. His father was a postal clerk. His mother raised her boys. And in those cramped quarters, it was Bill who remembered being the music kid.

Bill was just fifteen when he began writing a column called "The World of Rock" for the local weekly paper. He imported speakers from London. He even became a DJ. This seemed a natural step for him after discovering he was gay and living in New York in the early '70s. The Gay Activists Alliance held Saturday night dances at a firehouse in SoHo.

"It was like two dollars at the door and all the soda and beer you could drink, and there were really great DJs there, and somehow I got into doing some DJ'ing there as well. This was in the early days of club disco. Herbie Hancock's *Head Hunters* came out at the time. This was going on every Saturday night. We started doing some rock dances on Friday night, playing some glam rock or David Bowie or the Stones."

Ed led a far less glamorous life. He worked as a building superintendent during the 1970s. He got into the record business because of a girl. In 1978, he walked into Gina Franklyn's punk rock clothing shop on MacDougal Street.

Franklyn, born in London, had come to the States and partnered with sisters Tish and Snook to open Manic Panic, a boutique store that would become famous for its hair dye. But the sisters weren't really punk, she felt, and Franklyn decided to leave. She rented a space at 99 MacDougal in the Village for her own shop. It featured mainly punk rock fashions, but on her trips back to England, she would stop in to see Geoff Travis. He had started Rough Trade Records, first as a store, later as a label that put out Stiff Little Fingers, Scritti Politti, and, eventually, the Smiths.

"I would go over there and buy as many independent singles

as I could cram into my suitcase and I would sell them," said Franklyn. "Ed read about me owning the store and he came down the first or second day I opened. We talked and he asked me out to dinner and that's how the relationship started."

They expanded that relationship when Franklyn suggested Bahlman take over half of the store to sell records. Bahlman needed help. He found it in Terry Tolkin, who, years later, when Bahlman would all but disappear, would become a kind of de facto spokesman.

"He had to work a second job, busting his ass," said Tolkin, who never regretted the pay cut ($313 to $125 a week) he took by quitting his job as a file clerk at a law firm to work at 99. "He'd come straight from his maintenance job in his work overalls, all filthy, to open the store."

Bahlman also recruited his younger brother. He dropped a bunch of records off to Bill to entice him.

"It was kind of like, okay, it was a way of teasing me to whet my appetite to get involved in 99," said Bill Bahlman. "I listened to them and I was like, 'Wow, this is really amazing.' One of them was a group called Sham 69. He understood my passion for music and trusted me and all that stuff. Almost immediately, I said, 'Sure, I'd love to work with you.'"

• • •

Today, when everything is a click away, it's hard to understate the importance of 99 Records, but consider this. This was before Amazon, Discogs, eBay, Spotify, Pandora, or even the spread of Tower and Sam Goody. If you wanted something special—Augustus Pablo, Joy Division, the Buzzcocks—you needed to find somebody who traveled straight to the source and brought it back.

"It was impossible to locate any records," said Richard McGuire, a New Jersey kid who had moved to New York in the summer of 1979 and started the band that would become Liquid Liquid. "You'd just go through bins and look everywhere. It was a real treasure hunt. And sometimes, it's amazing the way things come to you, almost magical. I got the first Fela [Kuti] record I ever heard. A record called *Zombie*, which became one of the first touchstones for the band. I was listening to the Contortions. I'm listening to James Brown. We'd buy crazy things like Augustus Pablo instrumentals. We were listening to the Curtis Mayfield soundtrack that we may have bought for a dollar. And we were all living in the same place, this cheap place on Eightieth Street."

Well before Rubin got to NYU, Bahlman was helping him with his musical education—even if he didn't know it. Back in Long Island, Rubin was a loyal listener to Tim Sommer's radio show on WNYC, and he wrote Sommer a letter letting him know he was coming to the city for college. Bahlman sponsored that show.

"[Ed] didn't strike you as being a music fan, but he really was on top of everything," said Sommer. "Every week, he'd say, 'You have to hear this and this and this.' We tried to play the newest in music that nobody had played yet, and we were getting that stuff mainly from Ed and Terry."

99 was not the only store with imports.

Bleecker Bob's, just around the corner, was famous. Bob's was where Patti Smith met Lenny Kaye, *Village Voice* critic

Robert Christgau scrambled to grab the Clash's debut in 1977, and the Beastie Boys were famously thrown out, an incident they immortalized on 2004's "An Open Letter to NYC." But Bleecker Bob's was not for everyone.

"He had a reputation for being very confrontational," said Tolkin, who back then was working as a clerk at a law firm, but scouring record shelves in his free time. "He had the big, trained German shepherd behind the counter. And if he got mad at you, it's like, 'No soup for you.' Here's the record Nazi."

"Bleecker Bob's was the place where if you wanted to get sexually harassed as a young girl, that is where you would go," said Kate Schellenbach, who was the Beastie Boys drummer from 1981 to 1984, until they abandoned punk for hip-hop. "He was like an insult comic and not funny. I never bought records there."

"Bob was so nuts and paranoid," said Franklyn. "I had maybe twenty singles in the store that I brought from England, and he came over one day, yelling and screaming that what I was doing was trying to put him out of business. It was funny, because he was so nuts. I guess you could say, in a way, that Ed was everything Bleecker Bob wasn't."

"I hated going there," said McGuire. "Then I heard about 99. And Ed was a totally mellow guy and you could go there and he'd be happy to play records for you. He had a little turntable in the corner."

Rubin made his first trip to 99 when he was in high school. He ended up going by almost every day once he started at NYU. He would see Sommer there, who would eventually drop out of NYU and get a job at the newly founded MTV.

• • •

Around February 1980, Bahlman launched his label.

In one of the only interviews recorded of Bahlman, he tells Australian radio journalist Keri Phillips about meeting Richard Boon, who was managing the British punk band the Buzzcocks.

"I had just seen Glenn Branca at TF3, which is a small club where almost any band can play in and try new forms of music out, and I was really excited by what he was doing, but I had no formal plans to start a label and Richard Boon said, 'Why don't you just do it? Stop thinking about it. It only takes a couple of thousands of dollars to get going.'"

Branca, the cantankerous composer whose creative palette stretched from alternative theater to guitar symphonies, recorded his solo debut, *Lesson No. 1*, for Bahlman in 1980. Bahlman followed with a series of singles. He signed ESG, made up of the four Scoggins sisters and a friend. Their music would eventually be sampled by everyone from the Beastie Boys to TLC and the Wu-Tang Clan. Goldman's *Dirty Washing* was the fifth release, coming out in 1981.

Then there was McGuire's band, Liquid Liquid, who would sit at the center of the label's greatest success and the mythology surrounding its demise. McGuire had met Branca at a gig and learned about Bahlman's plans to put out his music. He was also dating one of the members of the three-girl band Ut. She told him 99 was going to release their record.

"I was like, 'Holy fucking shit,'" said McGuire. "That turned out not to be true, but it spurred me to give Ed a tape. He liked it, and he just said he'd like to see us play live. And we couldn't get a gig to save our souls. And we got us a gig at Pier 2. But Ed, once he saw us, he really got it. I remember him saying, 'Let's do a record.' And I was like, 'Holy crap, this really is happening.'"

Of the so-called no wave bands that arrived in the late '70s in New York, Liquid Liquid may have been the best. It wasn't their technique. In fact, the collective lack of command over their instruments is what may have led to their best work. They could jam for hours, settle on a groove and let it swim through an entire single. McGuire's bass lines were at the center of that sound and singer Sal Principato would moan and twist his vocal lines, often mumbling with a patter that was melodic, rhythmic, but unintelligible.

Their crowning moment came with "Caravan," a twisting dance track that 99 released in 1983.

The song became a huge club hit, so huge that Sugar Hill Records, never one to leave an easy theft on the table, grabbed its central groove for what would become one of hip-hop's signature songs, Grandmaster Melle Mel's "White Lines (Don't Do It)."

Rubin heard "Caravan" and came up with his own idea. He didn't have a record label yet, but he was developing his philosophy. He believed that different kinds of music could coexist, that you could love the Monkees and Kool Moe Dee. Rubin promoted a triple bill at the Hotel Diplomat with a hardcore band called Heart Attack, Moe's Treacherous Three, and Liquid Liquid.

"It seemed like inconceivable craziness," said McGuire. "This was, like, 1982. I remember the energy was very tense. People there for the hardcore stuff were onstage for that. They stepped back when the Treacherous Three came on. It felt uneven and strange. Just the fact that he was thinking to do that, I thought was brilliant."

• • •

When he started coming into 99, Rubin was "painfully shy, one of the shyest people I've ever met," said Tolkin.

That may be true, at least at first, but inside the basement store, Rubin could be at home.

Running a label, for Bahlman, was entirely hands-on. He and McGuire would make the rounds, in Bahlman's beat-up car, to record stores to deliver singles. The bassist remembered Rubin picking Bahlman's brain about how to press a record, distribute it, make labels.

"He was able to walk me through the process of this is a recording studio you can work at," said Rubin. "He would tell me where I could have record labels printed and where I could have sleeves printed, and if I had sleeves printed in Canada, they would be of a higher quality. Just each step of the process he would walk me through how to be able to do it. And the first two punk records I made, he distributed them for me because he had relationships with the different, independent distributors."

Hose had a dirty, distorted sound modeled more after the California-based Flipper than traditional hardcore groups. They mixed originals and unlikely covers—"You Sexy Thing" and Rick James's "Superfreak"—and eventually developed enough of a following to play gigs with the Meat Puppets and Hüsker Dü. When it came to putting out records, Rubin seemed to care as much, or even more, about the band's packaging as its music.

There would be two Hose singles. One came in a sleeve with a color scheme straight out of a Mondrian painting. The other slid into a brown paper bag and had song names scratched out in the vinyl center.

In those days, Rubin charted his album sales by making the rounds with Dubin. They'd stop for a chicken cutlet sandwich at St. Marks Place before scanning the bins at Rat Cage Records on Ninth Street.

"He'd say, 'I need to check my inventory,'" said Dubin. "He knew if I had dropped off five records and there were three, he would go up and ask for payment for his two records."

At night, they'd head to the clubs, an activity Dubin describes with a kind of awe. Whatever shyness Tolkin remembered emanating from that kid from Lido Beach, it seemed to be gone.

"We would go to the Roxy," said Dubin. "They actually had a gun check. You could come in and check your guns and knives. And we would go and see the rap acts. We went and saw the Treacherous Three. Rubin got fixated on bringing in Trouble Funk, the go-go band from D.C. It's a very tough act to bring in. There's seventeen guys in the band and bringing them all from D.C. There was nothing in it for him personally. He wanted to see them and he wanted to bring them to a New York audience. He was just completely divorced from the idea of making money. The other thing that was significant is that we'd go in, and within a minute, we'd walk through this crowd, and this was a heavily African American audience. If I looked up, within two minutes, Rubin was on the DJ stand with the DJ and they were laughing and talking. Even if Rick didn't know him, he would introduce himself and they'd start talking records. It was just weird. Sometimes we'd go to the World. Again, a really nasty neighborhood. We would go there, and there's a line to get in and Jazzy Jay is DJ'ing. We'd say, 'Rick, how are we going to get in?' He'd say, 'Watch this.' He goes over and finds Jazzy Jay's car on the street. It's like an Oldsmobile that's been pimped out a bit. He rattles a door handle and that would set off the alarm, which triggered a pager that Jazzy Jay had. Jazzy Jay comes out to see if someone is trying to bust into his car. He sees Rick and said, 'Okay, let's go in.'"

• • •

As Rubin got his bearings, one of his mentors started to lose his.

Things began to go very, very wrong at 99 Records.

By 1985, Ed Bahlman was a ghost, all but vanished, with Tolkin left behind as a kind of unreliable narrator of the label's brief history. Tolkin's post-99 career was impressive, as he signed a slew of critically acclaimed groups (Luna, Stereolab, Afghan Whigs) to Elektra Records. When it was over, when he'd moved to New Orleans to deal with his declining health, he would tell the amazing tale of Bahlman's demise—at least the version he wanted to tell—to zine writers, and watch as that account became adopted as a Wikipedia-stamped truth. On closer inspection, very little of Tolkin's story adds up.

So the tale: Bahlman sued Sugar Hill for stealing "Caravan" for "White Lines (Don't Do It)." As the case dragged on, Bahlman's life was threatened, the windows of 99 were smashed in, and, in one incident, guys with machetes showed up at the store to scare away customers. As Tolkin told it, Bahlman won in court, but it was a pyrrhic victory. By then, Sugar Hill had declared bankruptcy and refused to pay a dime. Bahlman, emotionally beaten and terrified, shut down his label and retreated.

A few problems with this sad tale.

There are no court records in New York or New Jersey of a case involving 99 and Sugar Hill. In addition, Bahlman dodged interviews about the label for decades.

I spent months trying to track him down. Every phone number listed for him over the years seemed to be disconnected. I found court papers showing he had briefly been married to the artist Lisa Krall in the mid-'90s. She did not take kindly to a call.

"I have no time to talk about this," Krall said before hanging up. "I hated Ed Bahlman. It was a mistake."

Bill Bahlman, so helpful when it came to the history of 99, thought Ed had worked at the post office after the record label's demise. Then he admitted that he and Ed hadn't talked in years. He wouldn't tell me why, and after that stopped taking my calls. As a last-ditch effort, I tried to trace Bahlman to his only public appearances post-99, a series of articles detailing how he and his partner, Anne-Katrin Titze, worked to protect the swans in Brooklyn's Prospect Park. There was even a 2011 photo of Bahlman in the *New York Times*, pinched, gray-haired, and unsmiling, as he stood near the water.

Titze, listed as a German professor and film critic, did not return e-mails or calls. So on a crisp afternoon, I headed to Prospect Park to see if I could get lucky. I asked an older couple taking photos by the water if they had seen Bahlman lately. The woman shook her head.

"Oh, I haven't seen them for a while," the woman said.

A few blocks over, I headed to the housing complex that was Bahlman's last stated address. A weather-beaten plate on the apartment door showed Bahlman's name. Nobody answered. I left a note but never got a reply.

Glenn Branca, for one, never bought Bahlman's story. He had a more cynical take, and did buy the Sugar Hill story.

"Here's the deal about Ed," said Branca only months before his death. "He took everybody's royalties and ran. As well as the master tapes. He was the most charming thief and bastard who ever stabbed anybody in the back. That's how he got away with it."

Franklyn had her own account of 99's demise. It was decidedly unglamorous, and again, wouldn't necessarily be the sort of story Bahlman could proudly tell to music historians.

"The final straw was that he had propositioned a girl who was working for me, and she didn't show up on a Saturday," said Franklyn. "I called her up and she said, 'Why don't you talk to Ed.' I was so infuriated. I don't think I was in love with Ed, but I was infatuated with him. I was in awe of him, I respected him, I knew he was supersmart, a razor-sharp mind. He could also be hurtful and cruel."

That day, Franklyn boxed up all her merchandise. She later opened up another store, called 99X.

Rick Rubin? He wouldn't ever see or talk to Bahlman again.

"He probably had learned everything he needed to learn," said Sommer. "He was astute enough to assess 99's limitations, plus realizing, 'I have a lot of big ideas and I'm not going to be able to accomplish my big ideas with these people.'"

For Rubin, the first of those big ideas would be sparked the spring day in 1983 when he came back to the dorm with a new 12-inch.

"I can remember, he walked in. 'This is the shit man, this is the shit,'" said Dubin.

The record? Run-DMC's "It's Like That" with "Sucker M.C.'s" on the B-side.

Chapter 13

DONE WITH *MIRRORS*

Geffen would be a fresh start, a rebirth. The boys had gone back on the road, proving on the Back in the Saddle tour that they could still fill arenas. Now it was time to head into the studio. So much had changed since Perry walked out. MTV, born as he rambled from club to club in that borrowed van, forced pop stars to rule the small screen, whether it was Prince crooning "When Doves Cry" in a bubble bath, ZZ Top turned into mystical truth-tellers with poodle guitars, or Michael Jackson recruiting Hollywood director John Landis for his fourteen-minute horror video, "Thriller." The gritty, '70s arena rock was giving way to a new genre—hair metal—as Bon Jovi, Ratt, and Cinderella cracked the *Billboard* charts. And even the great Eddie Van Halen, arguably the best player of his time or any time, had surrendered to the synthesizer. On the video for "Jump," the band's only number one hit, he plasters on a grin as he punches out a bloodless solo on an Oberheim OB-Xa designed for the masses.

On paper, at least, Aerosmith seemed to have a plan.

Jack Douglas would not be involved. In fact, he didn't even enter the discussion. The producer had been in a free fall since that night, in 1980, when he said good-bye to John Lennon after a recording session. They had made plans to meet, as always, for breakfast and to plot out the next day's session. Instead, the call came from the Dakota. John was gone, and the next day, Yoko asked Douglas to do what she couldn't, to serve as the public face of the family. You can see the video of him the night after, talking to Tom Snyder on TV, foggy about whether to use the past or present tense when it came to his idol, friend, and collaborator. And that would be it. Pills helped him sleep at first. Heroin came after. Sometime in the mid-'80s, Rick Dufay got a deal to make a record in London. He called his old friend and asked him to produce it.

"I'll meet you there," Douglas told him, and then never showed.

He wouldn't clean himself up for another decade and start working again until 1996, when he produced a Supertramp album.

In reality, Kalodner wouldn't have wanted Douglas anyway. He had just signed one of the biggest bands of the 1970s to Geffen. To move them forward, he needed somebody current, somebody hot, somebody with hits dripping off his résumé. He needed Ted Templeman.

What a coup. Templeman's track record spoke for itself. He started in the music business as the shaggy blond California kid who sang and played guitar in Harpers Bizarre, best known for their 1967 hit cover of Simon and Garfunkel's "The 59th Street Bridge Song (Feelin' Groovy)." By 1970, he had moved behind the board, working with everyone from Van Morrison and Carly Simon to Little Feat. Linda Ronstadt and David Geffen were pals of his. He dated singer Nicolette Larson, a Montana-born folk rock beauty who often sang with Ronstadt, and he produced her biggest hit, "Lotta Love." In 1980, Templeman, in a tux, accepted a Grammy for his work on the Doobie Brothers' hit "What a Fool Believes."

But Templeman's greatest discovery came on a rainy February night in 1977. That's when he walked into L.A.'s Starwood club and found a pair of Dutch brothers and a flamboyant singer with flowing locks blasting through an electrifying set in front of, at best count, eleven people. Templeman was hooked. He got Van Halen signed to Warner Bros. and produced their first six albums. It is his voice you hear during the famous spoken-word break in "Unchained," uttering, "Come on, Dave, give me a break."

"Ted Templeman was one of the great producers in the world," said Kalodner. "And he was on one of the big streaks of all time."

Only months before Templeman signed on for the Aerosmith record, Van Halen had released *1984*. The record updated the band's sound with synthesizers, landed them on MTV, and included "Jump," which would be the band's only number one single.

Perry and Tyler were impressed.

"That first record was awesome," said Perry. "Not that I wanted to sound like that, but I knew that Ted had the chops."

"Of course I listened to the Van Halen records, and I thought I knew what we were walking into," said Tyler. "And you always think the producer is going to bail you out and get a sound."

Kramer and Hamilton remembered the crunch of *Montrose*, the 1973 debut of the San Francisco power quartet featuring a twenty-five-year-old Sammy Hagar.

When a project succeeds, deviations in process, shifts from

routine, become elements of that success. When something goes wrong, every decision becomes a moment to second-guess. So the same Brian Wilson who playfully brought his dog into the studio to wrap up his classic *Pet Sounds* was the unhinged, melting-down rock star who made everyone wear fire helmets while recording a track on the aborted *Smile*.

Nothing quite so colorful took place on *Done with Mirrors*. At least, if anybody could remember those sessions. But from the start, something wasn't right.

First, Templeman found himself in unfamiliar surroundings. Normally, he'd do preproduction rehearsals in Los Angeles, his stomping ground. Instead, Aerosmith remained in Boston, where they could jam in the Wherehouse. Templeman flew in, and he went to dinner with the band. He went to a couple of Alcoholics Anonymous meetings with Tyler and Perry. (It was more a show of support than anything else. Templeman wouldn't stop using for years.) At the rehearsal space, the songs weren't all there, but what he heard was encouraging.

"I didn't realize how good they were," he said. "I was so knocked out with their musicianship. Joey Kramer is a monster drummer. Like a fucking metronome. Perry, you never knew where he was going, but his rhythm guitar playing, he had a certain rawness and magic to what he did. And Steven, he was so brilliant, I was almost intimidated."

The next step was bringing them into the studio. Again, Templeman had to adapt. He wanted to record at Sunset Sound in Los Angeles. Sunset was part of his routine. The studio was close to his office, so when Templeman was working with the Doobies or Van Halen, for example, he'd take the day's roughs and sit by himself, making notes as he listened to the tapes. He also knew the board and equipment better at Sunset. But Tim Collins made it clear that Sunset was out.

"He said, 'Listen, you can't record in L.A. because those guys will score,'" remembered Templeman. "'If you're in Oakland, Berkeley, they won't score.'"

"You know what, that's what they thought," Tyler said, laughing, years later. "You're asking me, why did they put Jesus on the cross? Well, that's what they thought. Sobriety stays with you. And you can get high anywhere you want."

Fantasy Studios, in Berkeley, was best known for its jazz recordings. Creedence Clearwater Revival had also recorded there, before Fantasy owner Saul Zaentz hit the band's leader, John Fogerty, with a nasty lawsuit.

Templeton immediately felt ill at ease.

"I wasn't used to the monitors, the mic preamp, any of it," he said. "I was like a fish out of water."

There was another problem with the producer, one he readily admitted later. His personal life was a mess. He remained married legally, but was involved with a woman across the country who happened to be engaged to a homicide detective. His drug use had escalated since he and his boys in Van Halen first did "krell," their code word for cocaine. (Aerosmith had their own secret word for blow: bleez.) In those days, drugs were as much a part of a music career as an overdub session. He remembered a night at the St. Francis Hotel with Doobie Brother Michael McDonald.

"They closed the bar at two o'clock or whatever, and they're vacuuming under us and we're just doing lines on the tables," he remembered. "But you know, everybody did that then. Someone's doing a bump everywhere you go. You go on a movie set and David Carradine would give you a bump. Nicolette and Linda, we all had it."

Collins was having his own problems, exacerbated by the Templeman situation. There wasn't a lot of money, yet the producer had a huge suite. Then he needed another. Collins heard he was having an affair with one of his assistants. Then maybe he was having an affair on the affair. Who knew?

"He was also doing a lot of blow, as was everybody else," said Collins. "And then at one point, the band walked out of the studio. I'm at the Claremont, just me and Steven. He was doing heroin. I was drinking. I was also binge-eating voracious amounts of food with Steven. I'm like, 'What the fuck.' Tom and Brad were like, 'We're out of here. You figure this out.'"

Collins, at this point, abandoned the band and took a friend's suggestion that he go to the Canyon Ranch treatment center in Tucson. He got sober on January 2, 1986, and, during that time, connected with Lou Cox, the clinical psychologist who would eventually treat the band.

But that was a ways down the road. As Templeman tried to capture Aerosmith, Kalodner began to realize he was headed toward failure. He had lost control of his record. Kalodner had always been clean. What he understood was the music. As the rough cuts came back to him, he began to worry. Nothing approached a single on this record. Maybe it was the best Aerosmith could do at the time. But it certainly wasn't the best of Aerosmith.

"I tried to talk to Ted Templeman or Tim, but I couldn't

really talk to Tyler or Perry. They were totally resistant," he said. "I don't think they understood what I did, and the discussion with them was kind of nonsensical. It was the exact opposite later on. At the time, it was like talking to somebody who didn't speak English and I didn't speak drugs."

It is not actually clear what kind of shape the so-called Bad Boys from Boston were in.

"I have very little memory of it, to be perfectly honest with you," said Kramer. "We didn't really have that much to do with one another. Everybody was pretty much doing their own things. I can only speak for myself. I was getting high. I had people bringing me things where we were."

Perry remembered showing up for recording sessions sober. He had promised Billie, who he married in 1985, that he wouldn't drink. He had begged off the harder stuff, though he concedes there were also times when he reached into his pockets and found them full of pills and powder.

"I think everybody wanted to be present," said Perry. "I was pretty clean, but I was a little bit white-knuckling it. You know, 'When the record's finished we'll take a break and go out and get tanked.'"

Later, there would be interventions and band therapy and a tell-all book meant to serve as a catharsis. (It actually led to more disagreements about where the truth lay.) But back then, the drugs and drinking, which everybody knew had helped bring them down, remained a subject best kept inside.

"I think that nobody wanted to be the one to admit they were having trouble," said Perry. "Whether or not the other guys were doing anything, I wouldn't know. But it wouldn't surprise me."

"It was a rough time," said Tyler. "We were all trying to stay sober, but we didn't know how. Music is the strongest drug, but we were used to, for ten years, writing music with the help of a shot of Jack. Why do you think they call it spirits? We were just kind of locked into this hotel together, and we just started pulling shit out of our asses. Like writing things like 'the reason a dog has so many friends because he wags his tail instead of his tongue.' It was just a time where we were digging deep. But like without a shovel. I feel like we were digging with our hands."

Perry brought "Let the Music Do the Talking," a song he'd recorded as the title track for the debut of the Joe Perry Project in 1980. It had a hook and driving rhythm revolving around Perry's slide guitar.

"I listened to it and said I didn't like the lyrics," said Tyler.

He rewrote them, and they at least had a single.

The pounding "My Fist Your Face" came out of Tyler's horrific stay at McLean Hospital in Belmont, Massachusetts. Tyler had done an ultimately failed rehab there before the recording.

"It was a locked ward. It was where they told me, 'Your best thinking got you here.' I ran back to my room and cried," he remembered.

The sessions proceeded. There were times when Templeman tried to trick the band from suffering from what Perry called the "red-light blues." He would put gaffer's tape on the recording light so that they thought they were rehearsing. He thought that would keep the sound fresh and raw. It did. But Perry wanted more guidance. Maybe "Fist" could have used some horns or a keyboard. Something.

"We were used to having a producer come in and help make it more cohesive," he said. "Like with Jack, we had riffs and pieces and he would help us cobble it together. Some of the songs on *Mirrors*, they're about eighty percent done."

Templeman loved Tyler. The singer would slip notes under his door at the hotel, sometimes with lyrics, sometimes with little jive slogans. And there was never a question that this was a rock and roll band. Late in the process, doing vocal overdubs with Tyler, Templeman and his engineer, Jeff Hendrickson, worked through a session straight out of *This Is Spinal Tap*. Or *Hammer of the Gods*.

Tyler brought a friend into the booth as he sang.

"If you soloed the mic, you'd hear the girl sucking his dick," said Templeman. "She was giving him head while he was doing the vocal. You know, it's hard to keep your composure through those types of things."

Nobody was happy as *Mirrors* came together. Kalodner heard the rough mixes and knew there still wasn't a single. Kramer, such a fan of Templeman's *Montrose* record, hated the sound of the drums.

"We got into this big argument," said Templeman. "After it was done, mastered. I just told him, 'It's done. It's mastered.' It's not like we just mixed the thing. I wouldn't say I let him down to you if I didn't think I had. I probably did. I just did the best I could."

The final indignity came with the album art. To title a record done by a band nearly finished by hard drugs *Done with*

Mirrors is questionable enough. Then came the design. Jeff Ayeroff, who had overseen dynamic album covers for the Police and Madonna, cooked up the idea of making all of the type backward. Not just the album title, but even the tiny credits on the inner sleeve.

"I was the only one that was opposed to putting everything on there backward," said Kramer. "I thought that was the dumbest idea I ever heard."

"Somebody should have smacked us," said Tyler. "We sat around saying, 'Yeah, that's going to be so cool, and everybody will have to read the credits by looking in the mirror.' Like, who the fuck is going to hold an album up to a mirror? They're too busy snorting blow off a mirror."

"It goes to show you the general level of insanity and incompetence surrounding that record," said Kalodner. "That I even allowed that cover to happen. It's also my fault it even got that far."

"Let the Music Do the Talking" came out in September, barely cracking the Top 20. *Done with Mirrors* arrived two months later. It remains the lost Aerosmith record, not a bad album if you consider the era during which it emerged. There are no cheesy synths, no celebrity cameos, none of the slickness that defined the mid-'80s. But what ultimately defined *Mirrors* was one other element it didn't have. Hits. The record peaked at thirty-six on the *Billboard* charts. Aerosmith was suddenly less popular than Mr. Mister. Their comeback album would need eight years to sell the 500,000 copies required to go gold.

David Geffen gave Kalodner, once his golden boy, a directive. Fix this situation with Aerosmith or you're done.

"He said to me, 'If you make one more record like this, I'm

going to fire you,'" remembered Kalodner. "And he didn't say it in a calm way. There's only two times he ever spoke to me not in a calm way. That was one of them. He just said, 'Why is this such a terrible record? You had all these hits.' I said, 'I tried my best,' and I remember this classic David Geffen line, why he's the smartest person I ever met. He said, 'Don't try, do.'"

Chapter 14
"THE REDUCER"

It's no surprise that Rick Rubin's first choice for his new label would be the Treacherous Three. They were favorites, and also a prime example of what he felt was wrong in the world of recorded hip-hop. At Harlem World or the Fever, Kool Moe Dee, LA Sunshine, and Special K could blow your face off. In the studio, they were often discofied into submission. Bobby Robinson's Enjoy label had put out a series of singles, including "Feel the Heartbeat" and "The Body Rock." Those were okay. Then the Three got signed to Sugar Hill and the rhymes softened, the orchestrations grew cheesier. Nothing they had committed to vinyl approached the energy of a Treacherous Three gig.

The idea sounded perfect until Rubin met with Moe in his dorm room and pitched him on Def Jam. As much as he would've loved to work with him, Moe said he couldn't. The Treacherous Three were signed to an exclusive deal with Sugar Hill. But Moe suggested Rubin talk to Special K. He heard he had a brother who could rap.

That was Clarence "Terry" Ronnie Keaton, another kid from the Bronx. Keaton may not have been as well known as his younger brother, but he could command the mic. He also took special pride in telling everyone that he had been there, that night in 1973, when Kool Herc hosted hip-hop's coming-out party at 1520 Sedgwick. As he moved through high school,

Keaton began to dance and MC, first as T and later as T La Rock. He wasn't desperate for a deal, though, and wasn't bowled over when Rubin called.

"I was working at a nice, cushy job at a pharmacy," said Keaton. "Rapping and DJ'ing on the side. But we spoke on the phone for a while and I said, 'The least I can do is go meet Rick.'"

Special K, Keaton, and his DJ, Louie Lou, headed to University Place for a meeting in room 712. They were greeted by Rubin and Adam Horovitz.

Horovitz had entered Rubin's life earlier in 1983 after his band, the Beastie Boys, put out their obnoxiously entertaining single "Cooky Puss." It mixed the audio of a prank call Horovitz made to Carvel, inventors of the aforementioned ice cream cake character, over a soft-hop beat.

When they'd formed in 1981, the Beasties had been a hardcore band, a four-piece that included drummer Kate Schellenbach. But their increasing fascination with hip-hop eventually led them to Rubin's dorm room. He had those turntables and a bubble machine.

"We were like, 'If we had a fucking DJ and a fucking bubble machine, we'd be fucking killing it,'" Horovitz remembered years later.

Before long, Horovitz was a fixture in 712, tending to the demo tapes flowing into Weinstein Hall's mail room. And the Beasties were adding a hip-hop set to their gigs, bringing out DJ Double R to work the turntables. The guys connected with Rubin. Schellenbach didn't.

"He was a dick and kind of a sexist asshole," she said. "He said to me, 'I don't like the way women sound rapping.'"

That summer, Schellenbach went away to Europe for a few weeks. When she returned, she ran into the rest of the group: Horovitz, Mike Diamond, and Adam Yauch. They were dressed in ridiculous, matching Puma tracksuits. Rubin had one, too. It was clear she was out.

"Adam Yauch came up to me and said, 'Rick thinks we could be the first all-white rap band,'" Schellenbach remembered.

Rubin made an immediate impression on Keaton. In the dorm room, Keaton noticed the Roland TR-808 sitting on the pair of desks Rubin had pushed together. As far as Keaton knew, one of the only other people with an 808 was Afrika Bambaataa, who had used that very drum machine for "Planet Rock" back in 1982.

Rubin already had a beat in mind. He put it on a tape and gave it to Keaton. And that's when DJ Louie Lou lost his chance to land himself in the hip-hop history books. On the way home, Lou got into an argument with Special K over that tape. He wanted to take the tape home. Special K wanted his brother, who had to rehearse his rap, to have it.

"I said, 'You all are acting like children,'" remembered Keaton. "My brother said, 'I don't want Louie coming down anymore and I don't want Louie on the record. This is my brother.' So we told Rick and he said, 'Okay, we have somebody who is going to come in and perform scratches.' He mentioned Jazzy Jay."

Rubin had first watched DJ Jazzy Jay work at Negril on Second Avenue, one of the few places you could see hip-hop without heading to the Bronx or Harlem. Jay was a member of Universal Zulu Nation, the street gang turned cultural collective created by

Bambaataa. He would become not only a friend. He'd be the one to wire up Rubin's MGB with a custom monster speaker system.

Late in 1983, T La Rock, Rubin, and Jazzy Jay gathered at Power Play Studios in Queens. Rubin had recorded his own band, Hose, there, largely because the studio charged only $45 an hour. They needed three hours to lay down "It's Yours."

It is a joyous track, opening with a series of scratches, hand claps, and Keaton's smooth rhymes.

Commentating, illustrating
Description giving, adjective expert
Analyzing, surmising, musical
Myth-seeking people of the universe, this is yours!

"We were all crowding around the engineer," said Keaton. "The 808 is a natural bass machine. And I'm sitting there, and I kept telling the engineer, 'Put more bass.' And he's looking at me like I'm crazy. And one of the Beastie Boys was saying, 'Yeah.' That's why 'It's Yours' is really considered the first real bass record."

That night, Horovitz drank Brass Monkey for the first time, a nasty, premixed cocktail that was part beer, part orange juice. It would eventually become the title and subject of a song on the Beastie Boys' debut album two years later. On "It's Yours," Dave Scilken, his best friend from high school, was part of the small group that shouted the "Yeahs" in the call-and-response with T.

Do you like it?
Yeah.
Do you want it?

Yeah.
Well, if you had it would you flaunt it?
Hell, yeah.
Well, it's yours.

"I was blown away," remembered Keaton. "I love beats. When I heard that record it was like nothing I'd heard and nothing that was out at the time."

Russell Simmons felt the same way.

Thirty-two years later, he sat in his office and launched into the first line.

"'Commentating, illustrating / Description giving, adjective expert,'" he said. "I heard that and I was like, 'Holy shit.'"

"It's Yours" came out in January 1984. It wasn't until July that Simmons met Rubin at the party for *Graffiti Rock*, the Michael Holman pilot meant to be a kind of hip-hop version of *American Bandstand*. Run-DMC appeared in the episode, as did Kool Moe Dee and Special K. Rubin and Simmons began to hang out. They went to clubs together. They visited Rubin's dorm room, where he showed Simmons his drum machine.

"I heard beats, one after another, that was phenomenal," said Simmons. "Every beat was a record. Put the right rapper on the beat, that's a record. And then beyond that, he was able to do much more. But just hearing those records on his machine made me inspired."

Rubin, for his part, was also impressed. This wasn't some NYU classmate he'd harangued into going to Danceteria after a box of General Tso's chicken. This was a real producer, promoter, a guy from the business. Simmons had made some of the records Rubin loved: Jimmy Spicer's "The Bubble Bunch," Orange Krush's "Action," and, best of all, "Sucker M.C.'s."

"I was a kid in college," Rubin said. "He was Russell Simmons, which, even though it was a very small pond, he was a big fish in that very small hip-hop pond even then."

Technically, Def Jam began in 1982 when Rubin put out a single by his punk band, Hose. Great care went into the appearance of that record, from the song titles scratched into the vinyl center to the paper bag in which it was inserted. But Ed Bahlman's 99 Records had distributed the Hose record, so it wasn't technically Rubin's label.

T La Rock's debut would be different. For the release, Rubin handed a sketch to his sort-of girlfriend, Gretchen Viehmann—they'd gone on dates and she'd met Mickey and Linda, she said, yet they had no physical relationship—a sketch he'd done of the logo he wanted to create for Def Jam. It showed a tonearm and the familiar oversized *D* and *J* meant to emphasize the most important part of a Def Jam release, the DJ.

It was a start. Still, even if Rubin got the art right, he had Arthur Baker's Partytime label put out "It's Yours." It would be the last Def Jam recording released by somebody else.

• • •

James Todd Smith was in a roller rink in Queens that night in 1983 when he first heard "Sucker M.C.'s." He was just fifteen, but Smith had been rapping since fifth grade, joined a group called the Disco Deuce at eleven, and won $200 in a contest at Pete's Place in Hollis at thirteen.

"I actually thought somebody was up on the mic rapping,

and I was kind of dismissive of it," he said. "'Cause I was competitive. But then, once I realized it was a record and I listened to it more and more and more, I became a die-hard fan."

The sound was obviously different. Stripped down, an antidote to Sugar Hill. Then Smith saw a picture of Run-DMC with their leather coats and unlaced sneakers. The look matched the sound. Forget the feathered hats and Studio 54 suits.

"Basically, they're the ones that brought the street to hip-hop," Smith said. "I wouldn't say they the first ones, because there were other guys that did it, too. Like Cowboy from the Furious Five. And a few other guys that were really street. But they were the first ones that embraced the street completely as a group in terms of the aesthetics and the execution. Not just the urban environment. It was like a direct line. We rap over the breakbeats, the drum loops when we're at the block party or at the party in the park. We going to rap over a drum loop on the record. We rap with Adidas on and our baggy jeans on and our stuff on when we're in the park, we're going to wear that at the concert."

It was early the next year, just after his sixteenth birthday, that Smith heard "It's Yours."

There was one huge difference between T La Rock's debut and "Sucker M.C.'s." Rubin put the Weinstein Hall address—5 University Place, Room 712—on the record sleeve.

"I still remember the phone number on it," said Smith. "It was very important. So I sent the demo in and then I called him all the time and I bugged him and bugged him until Ad let him hear the tape and called me in."

He was billing himself as Ladies Love Cool James and, after

hearing from Horovitz, took the subway down to University Place. Rubin came down to meet him at the Weinstein front desk. Like most everyone, LL was surprised. Rubin was white. Then they went to the room and cut "I Need a Beat" right there to be a song on the demo tape.

Rubin and LL went to work on *Radio*, the album that would make him a star. Years later, Run and D would discuss how much credit—too much credit—they thought Rubin got for *Raising Hell*. LL wouldn't raise any of those questions. Rick Rubin, credited as "the reducer" on the back cover, was a godsend for him. They wouldn't work together long. Rubin headed off to California. LL recruited other producers. But their collaboration on his debut record was key.

"Oh, man. Rick basically guided me through that process. Held my hand through that process. I would make records. I could hum a beat to Rick or drum patterns to him with my mouth and he would re-create them with the 808 machine. Every time we would make a song, when he would call me back in a few days he would play something over the phone and it would be completely different. It would be like an amazing surprise. He did all the drum programming and everything. There were no ghost programmers, no ghost writers, just me and Rick."

LL's debut marked the start of something special. The artist would become arguably the most successful rapper of all time, retaining his recording career even as he became a television star. He would be the first rapper awarded a Kennedy Center honor.

But for Rubin, LL's arrival sparked something else. It marked the start of his partnership with Simmons. Whenever they may have verbally agreed to go into business together, the pair made their official announcement with a piece in *Billboard* magazine in its November 17, 1984, issue. The article reported that L.L. Kool (sic) J's "I Need a Beat" would be Def Jam's first single with Jimmy Spicer and the then unknown Beastie Boys, "a group of white rockers who rap over heavy metal rhythms," also on the label.

Rubin explained the logic of the partnership to Bill Adler years later when Def Jam marked its twenty-fifth anniversary by publishing a coffee-table book.

"I just finished this record," Rubin told Simmons. "What should I do with it? And he said, 'It's great, it's a hit, let's give it to Profile.' And I said, 'Since we've been friends, all you've done is complain to me about Profile. About how you hate 'em and how they steal from you and they don't pay you and they don't do stuff . . . Why would we give it to them?' And he said, 'Well, there's so few options.' And I said, 'Well, why don't we just do it ourselves! . . . I'll make all the records, I'll do all the work. I'll do everything. You just be my partner.'"

Chapter 15
CHOOSING "WALK"

The album was finished, everyone agreed, and yet Rick Rubin couldn't shake the feeling something was missing. It was more than a song. Rubin found himself getting almost philosophical as he considered the state of hip-hop in 1986. It wasn't merely that so many misunderstood it. What frustrated Rubin most is how many smart people didn't even view it as music. The missing piece would be the connector in the erector set of his musical imagination.

"I was looking for a way to bridge that gap in the story of finding a piece of music that was familiar and already hip-hop friendly so that on the hip-hop side it would make sense and on the non-hip-hop side you'd see it wasn't so far away," he said.

He wouldn't find any resistance at Profile. Cory Robbins wasn't necessarily searching for ways to introduce the art form to a wider audience. His reasons for wanting to crash through the rap ceiling were more practical.

"It was impossible to get them played on pop radio," Robbins said. "Not hard. Not even in the realm of possibility."

The idea of melding rock and rap wasn't foreign territory for Rubin. In 1984, he had sampled the central riff of AC/DC's "Back in Black" for "Rock Hard," the debut Def Jam single from the Beastie Boys. One night early in 1986, Rubin called up Tim Sommer, the former NYU radio jock, and told him, "I need a white rock song that can be turned into a rap song."

"And we spent about ten or fifteen minutes on the phone, shooting around ideas," said Sommer. "We kept on coming back to 'Back in Black' by AC/DC, but the Beastie Boys had recorded a version. Then Rick goes, 'How about "Walk This Way"?' And he begins to sing it on the phone, with imitation scratches. At this point, I go, 'Rick, that's a fantastic idea,' but I said, 'You know you have to get Steven Tyler and Joe Perry to play on it.' And Rick said, 'They'll never do it. Old white guys don't get this rap thing.' I said, 'I work at MTV News. They've just reunited. Their reunion isn't going all that well.'"

Strangely enough, that's not the only account of how Aerosmith and Run-DMC came together. In 2010, Sue Cummings, a onetime *Spin* editor—and Sommer's former girlfriend—wrote a short piece for the magazine with the headline: "*Spin* Introduces Run-DMC to Aerosmith."

In that piece, Cummings claims she was the one who thought of the idea.

"I called Rick Rubin," Cummings wrote. "'Can you give me a tape of Run-DMC? I'm going to Boston to meet Aerosmith.' 'That would be *incredible*!' he replied.

"When I met up with the band, I proposed the collaboration. Aerosmith had never heard of Run-DMC when I handed them that cassette, but they were willing to take the risk of working with a new artist."

Years later, Cummings conceded that everyone could be right. She and Sommer and Rubin were close and spent a lot of time together, whether going to see Anthrax or Slayer at L'Amour or just chatting.

"Back then, we would talk on the phone every day," she said. "I talked to Tim. I talked to Rick. I don't dispute that Tim suggested it to him, but I suggested it to him, too. It might have been that Tim and I thought of it."

Whoever actually suggested the idea, it clearly made sense in Rubin's sonic imagination. He wasn't interested in the kind of flashy hair-metal licks that had become popular with Def Leppard, Bon Jovi, and Quiet Riot. He had, in fact, grumbled to Sommer about the guitar sound on "Rock Box" and "King of Rock." His vision wasn't to simply mix rap and rock. Technically, Kurtis Blow did that back in 1980 with his weirdly off-key croon of Bachman-Turner Overdrive's "Takin' Care of Business."

"It's one thing to say, 'We're going to mix rap and rock,'" said Sommer. "That wasn't his vision. His vision was mixing rap and this heavy riffing that one gets from Sabbath or Blue Öyster Cult or Aerosmith. That's very different. What Rick said is, 'I'm going to take this definitively unfunky white music and I'm going to take that and mix that with rap.' That was the experiment of the Beasties and to a lesser extent the experiment of Run-DMC. It's an oversimplification to say mixing rap and rock. Anybody can do that. What Rick wanted was a specific kind of rock. That meathead kind of rock."

Aerosmith had been one of Rubin's favorites in high school. He followed them closely enough to go see the Joe Perry Project play live in 1979. He even made an aborted attempt to help the reunited band record a few new songs. (A bootleg of those sloppy demos, *Love Me Like a Bird Dog*, suggests they were done in early 1987, though everybody involved believes it was before "Walk This Way." No records of the session seem to exist.)

To get "Walk" rolling, Rubin decided to call Aerosmith's representative at Geffen to pitch his idea.

John Kalodner was no normal record company exec. He had started his work career by running a record store in his native Philadelphia in the early '70s before getting work as a music critic for the *Philadelphia Bulletin*, the city's evening paper, and eventually for the morning *Inquirer*. Then came his true calling. In 1974, Atlantic Records hired Kalodner to work in their publicity department and, before long, he found his way to artists and repertoire, where he pushed the label to sign Foreigner and AC/DC.

By 1986, Kalodner was a kind of insider star, known as much for his golden touch with bands as for his look—the white suits, thick beard, and sunglasses made famous by John Lennon. Kalodner's disinterest in drugs also set him apart. He didn't need any chemicals to inspire self-confidence. On records he influenced, Kalodner claimed a special title starting with Foreigner's 1978 self-titled debut:

John Kalodner: John Kalodner.

By the time Rubin called, David Geffen, famous for launching the Eagles, Linda Ronstadt, Jackson Browne, and Joni Mitchell on Asylum Records in the 1970s, had launched a new label, Geffen Records. In 1980, he hired Kalodner as the first artists and repertoire executive.

There were successes, particularly Asia, but his signing of the reformed Aerosmith was not turning out to be one of them.

As the summer of 1986 rolled around, even the slickest publicist couldn't have spun *Done with Mirrors* into anything less than a bomb. The album opened June at 190 on the *Billboard* 200. What's worse, *Classics Live*, a sluggish smorgasbord released by Columbia as part of Aerosmith's exit deal, hovered in the Top 100. The compilation had such murky provenance that the record company didn't list which tracks featured Crespo and Dufay.

Kalodner, the bearded A&R guru, suddenly found himself in an unlikely spot: worried about his job. Then Rubin called.

It sounded intriguing, and sometime during the winter of 1986, Kalodner decided to stop by Def Jam's office to hear out the young producer. He admits he wasn't expecting to find that Rubin's headquarters was a dorm room.

"It looked like a bum slept there, and here's this guy who looks like some young schlub," said Kalodner. "Except he spoke so clearly and he had such a clear vision of what he wanted to do."

Kalodner knew nothing about rap. He wasn't about to pretend he did. But as famous as he would become for pushing what he described as "corporate rock"—groups like Aerosmith, Nelson, and Whitesnake—he wasn't above appreciating an innovative musical idea that cut against the grain. He did, after all, sign XTC and Siouxsie and the Banshees. He also had some questions for Rubin.

"I think I said to him, 'Do the schwarzes even know who Aerosmith is?'" remembered Kalodner, invoking a Yiddish word that's either derogatory (at best) or racist (at worst). "I don't know if I'm proud of it, but it's what I said to Rick."

Then he told him he thought it was a great idea. He did wonder whether it could work.

"I thought in my head, 'Good luck to you working with two people who are higher than a kite,'" said Kalodner.

The next call went to Collins. Kalodner needed Aerosmith's manager on his side. He also needed Collins to talk to the band.

The manager admits he was as clueless as Kalodner. It could be a great idea or it could be a disaster. He deferred to the record exec and presented the idea. Reaction, as he remembered it, was mixed. Tyler immediately sounded game. Today, he talks of the early '80s, living at the Gorham Hotel with his twenty-dollar-a-day allowance.

"I loved rap," he said. "I used to go looking for drugs on Ninth Avenue and I would go over to midtown or downtown and there would be guys on the corner selling cassettes of their music. I'd give them a buck, two bucks, and that was the beginning of me noticing what was going on in New York at the time."

Whitford, Hamilton, and Kramer were down on the idea. At least that's what Collins and Kalodner remembered. Over time, the record executive has taken to referring to them dismissively as the LI3, or the less important three.

"They were always against everything," Kalodner said. "They were against doing 'I Don't Want to Miss a Thing.'"

But Hamilton, looking back, didn't remember having any reservations about Run-DMC.

"I definitely had a feeling of being left out," he said.

"Like, can't we all go?" Whitford added.

But Rubin only needed two. He had Tyler. He also needed

Perry. The guitarist wasn't necessarily against the pitch. He just wasn't sure. Then, a thirteen-year-old kid with a growing collection of cassettes entered the conversation.

Perry's divorce from Elissa had gone through and, during the making of a video for the Project's last-ditch third record, he had met Billie Paulette Montgomery, a model who didn't know a thing about Aerosmith. They began to date, and got married in 1985.

It was her son, Aaron, who found himself providing guidance to Perry one day.

"Joe was curious," Billie remembered. "He went into Aaron's room and asked him about it. Aaron was trying to show him how you break-dance. Aaron got into it as much as a Jewish white kid could. He rolled around on the floor and kicked his feet up."

"I was so into rap," said Aaron. "I've always had an eclectic taste in music, because growing up, my mom was a young mom and she knew a lot of artists, musicians around the area. She was more into the punk rock scene. I got turned on to a lot of college radio. That's where I would hear Doug E. Fresh, the Sugarhill Gang, and that first Run-DMC album."

Perry also had reservations about the band's fans. Maybe they wouldn't get it. But there was a certain logic to it. He grew up with the blues.

"I heard a direct connection between what they were doing and the blues," he said. "All you had to do was have a boom box and some talent. And a way to express yourself, which is what they were doing, on the street corner. Which is what blues was. They'd be on the street in the day or in the juke joint at night. They were singing about living wherever they were living, and to me, it was like a direct connection."

The one thing missing, Perry would say later about his stepson's rap tapes, was easy for him to get his hands on. The only thing missing: his guitar.

Chapter 16

THE LEVEE

So did they even need it? Perhaps a strange question to ask so many years later. Punch up any streaming service and "Walk This Way" is at the top of every Run-DMC playlist. The song's significance in pop culture is undeniable, whether watching the climatic closing scene of *Ray Donovan* or the ladies dressing up in *Sex in the City*. There is a reason "Walk" and not "Sucker M.C.'s" or "Peter Piper" is on the new *Smithsonian Anthology of Hip-Hop and Rap*.

The hot take, of course, is to dismiss "Walk" as a cheap money-grab, another example of the commercial (aka white mainstream) watering down the authentic. Pat Boone redoing Little Richard. Howlin' Wolf pushed to record with British rockers half his age. The Fat Boys and Chubby Checker.

Except that "Walk This Way" is so many things to so many different people, from bar mitzvah boys in Westchester County to Ice-T.

It brings together two very distant universes—the B-boys from Hollis, the (white) bad boys from Boston—if only for a few hours on a Sunday. It's also the starting gun for every mash-up, good and bad, that came later. Public Enemy and Anthrax. Puff Daddy and Jimmy Page. Rage Against the Machine. Kid Rock. Limp Bizkit. All of them came after "Walk," as did *Yo! MTV Raps*, Arsenio, and the first black president.

But back to the other side. To that other crowd—the ones who don't recognize "Rapper's Delight" as the first hip-hop song, who don't consider Rick Rubin the king, or even a decorated prince, of rap—"Walk" is something less than revolutionary. It's a sellout, and it's also no coincidence that, by 1986, when it was recorded, Larry was gone, replaced by Rick Rubin. And he wasn't the only white guy now in the room. Lyor Cohen was running the road show, his future a brightly lit path straight to the top at Warner Music. Bill Adler, a white, Jewish guy with an ever-present beard, served as minister of information, adviser, photo collector, and eventually the ultimate authority on a decade never to be forgotten.

Adler had spent the 1970s bouncing between free-form radio stations and journalism. He met Simmons in 1983 when he was writing a story about *Dance Fever* for *People* magazine. The next year, Simmons hired him for a job that morphed into director of publicity for Def Jam.

"There was nobody like me," said Adler. "He was open to white people."

"He was open to white people, yes," said Bill Stephney, the Adelphi University programmer also hired by Simmons, "but also the notion of African American artists having an in-house publicist. I don't think Luther Vandross had in-house publicity. Or Freddie Jackson, or even Anita Baker at that point. Which is why you always say Run-DMC or Whodini. What are they doing on the cover of *Rolling Stone*? Why are they at Live Aid? Why are they there with Madonna and the Rolling Stones when the Boogie Boys had a number one record with 'Fly Girl,' but you don't even know what they look like?"

Some saw the influx of outsiders into the Rush and Def Jam offices as a threat.

Talib Haqq, known as Trevor "Butchie" Greene back in the day, used to snap pictures during his days at Rush. He took the photos on Run-DMC's self-titled debut.

"Russell, he needed to make an allegiance with Jews," said Haqq. "A smart goal, but at the end of the day, he stepped on a lot of niggas. Russell's plan was to make his alliance with people outside his tribe. So Larry was his first victim."

Others don't buy it.

"It's an alliance with Jews?" said Dan Charnas, the author of *The Big Payback*, who worked with Rubin at Def American. "Rick Rubin, a powerless fucking college student who has a little bit of talent. Lyor, who had no power until Russell brought him in. Russell's the power. Russell's the genius. Russell made all these things happen."

When the question was brought up, Stephney would tell the story of the first time he spoke to Simmons. It was the fall of 1982, and he had been assigned a freelance piece on Kurtis Blow for a magazine called *New York Rocker.* When he finally reached Simmons, he remembered that he scribbled his name down as Simons.

"He sounded like an ethnic New Yorker, probably had a bar mitzvah in Queens," said Stephney. "At the same time, he probably thought I was a midwesterner who freelanced for the *Voice.* You had these two black guys in the middle of hip-hop who thought each other were white on the other side."

Simmons, Stephney knew, had hung out with a pretty diverse group of friends even back in Hollis. That dynamic didn't change when he started Rush and partnered with Rubin on Def Jam.

"Trust me, many of us brothers who have run labels and companies have all wished for a Lyor and a Bill Adler, and could not find them," he said.

Heidi Smith, who started at Rush as Simmons's executive assistant and rose to become Def Jam's director of video production, described the atmosphere of the company as one where skin color didn't make a difference. Rush was, in her description, a "teaching college."

"We had people from everywhere," she said. "It was obviously not just something that was happening on records, it was a lifestyle. So it was just a very all-inclusive atmosphere. People you would never think would be sitting together at a party. Some guys in suits. Some guys with long hair. And a bunch of rappers. It was a movement."

• • •

Even if Larry Smith himself didn't seem to harbor a heavy resentment toward Simmons, it is important to consider race as it relates not just to "Walk This Way," but to Run-DMC in general. It doesn't always work the way you might expect. Simmons said much of the record company resistance came from black, not white, executives, terrified of appearing too uncivilized by pushing "street music."

Run couldn't ignore race when he considered "Walk This Way."

He remembered not playing the song at concerts early in 1986, when "My Adidas" and other *Raising Hell* tracks were already part of the playlist. He also didn't perform it when he did solo gigs, years later, at the famed New York City hip-hop club the Tunnel.

"Because it's a fully black crowd that wants to hear 'Peter Piper' only," he said. "If I'm going to make them jump up and down at this fully black club, 'Walk This Way' will not go over well."

"'Walk This Way,'" he maintained, "was a separate thing in my mind."

Lyor Cohen had even stronger feelings.

"I hated the record," said Cohen. "In fact, I would always leave the arena or performance when they would start to play it."

Back on the day it was recorded, Cohen didn't raise his voice in protest. In fact, in the footage MTV took that day, Cohen looks thrilled and awed to be in the room. He's a scruffy kid of twenty-six, and he's bopping and smiling as Joe Perry lays down his track.

Years later, after running Def Jam and then Warner Bros. music itself, he remained tantalized by the question of what would have happened had Run-DMC *not* recorded "Walk This Way."

"It was becoming more and more obvious that what Run-DMC and what rap music was doing was special," said Cohen. "Like the levee was about to break. I did not want a concocted, white, obvious thing to break the levee. The levee was being broken by urban expression."

The song also didn't do Run-DMC any favors, Cohen believed. It was a layup for the media to finally connect the dots. If only it were more authentic, he felt.

"They needed a vessel, they needed a moment, they needed

a song, to put it all in context," he said. "I wanted to extend the urban little secret. I started seeing more and more white people intrigued by the art form as it was growing and didn't need to pop them on the head with a sonically obvious record that, in my mind, felt dishonest."

Not only that, but "Walk This Way" marked the beginnings of the hairline fracture of Run-DMC.

"We were like a powerful little secret running through America. The established music business rejected rap music, and media was slow to come. And we had a nice, little powerful, very successful urban and exciting art form that was pleasing a lot of kids. And then came 'Walk This Way,' which in my mind was jumping to the third act and skipping the second act. Unfortunately, after the third act, the curtain falls."

• • •

That's hindsight. Back then, Cohen admitted, he was the road manager, no record mogul. It would have been strange for him to speak up in the studio.

"My eyes were on my feet," he said.

In 1986, Russell Simmons, Profile Records, and Run-DMC were not thinking much about the "levee," and the natural, organic way to bust over it. They were trying to sell records. And they were at a serious disadvantage when up against forgettable milquetoast artists like Mr. Mister or A-ha. The two main hit drivers were mainstream radio and MTV. The two main hit drivers did not play hip-hop.

That may be impossible to imagine today, when hip-hop occupies virtually every corner of our culture, from commercials to fashion to soft drinks to soundtracks. But in 1985, even after Run-DMC's *King of Rock* landed in the *Billboard* 200 for fifty-six weeks and earned a four-star review in *Rolling Stone*, Lyor Cohen and Bill Adler were rebuffed when they submitted a treatment for an episode of the popular *Cosby Show.*

The show, produced decades before its star would be publicly exiled after a slew of sexual assault allegations and a conviction, was considered revolutionary for its portrayal of African Americans. *The Cosby Show* was also a huge mainstream hit, the top-rated sitcom on television for five of its eight seasons.

What Cohen and Adler wrote up sounds like a perfect plot-by-the-numbers episode. Theo Huxtable—the teenage son played by Malcolm-Jamal Warner—has become a huge Run-DMC fan, has joined the group's fan club, and is met with resistance from his TV father, Cliff Huxtable, played by Bill Cosby. The elder Huxtable looks at a Run-DMC poster on the wall and declares them gangsters. "But, Dad, there's a message in their music," pleads Theo. "Right! And the next thing you're gonna tell me is that it's music, too," Cliff responds. In the treatment, Run and D end up visiting the Huxtable home and winning over the patriarch by talking about the importance of school, hard work, and family. Then Cliff and the guys rap out a few lines. The treatment, dated September 4, 1985, was returned unread.

Then the following April, after *King of Rock* had gone platinum, Run-DMC sent a tape to NBC's popular *Late Night with David Letterman*. In 1989, after the breakthrough success of "Walk This Way," Letterman bandleader, Paul Shaffer, would release a solo album that featured Will Smith, and bring the rapper and future film star onto *Late Night* to perform with him.

But in 1986, the show's talent coordinator politely declined the group's request to perform on the show.

"We viewed the tape in a recent talent meeting and even though they are very talented we do not feel they fit our format," Sandra Furton, the talent coordinator, wrote.

Which is why even if Run-DMC, singular stars already, didn't necessarily need "Walk This Way," hip-hop itself did. By tapping into the classic rock canon and surrendering the chorus to Steven Tyler's distinctive howl, the song basically served as hip-hop's Trojan horse, the music camouflaged enough to give timid programmers permission to play.

Oedipus, the influential program director of Boston's WBCN, explained the issue dispassionately. The decision to stick to adult-oriented rock was not personal. It was not racism.

"We didn't care if artists were black or white," he said. "We were not a rap station."

With "Walk This Way," they didn't have to flip formats. The music did the job for them.

Chapter 17

MARCH 9

There was nothing exceptional about the way the weekend started, nothing to foreshadow what would go down that Sunday. That history would be made.

Aerosmith's Saturday night gig in Philly went smoothly. No collapses. No fights. Ted Nugent, the opener, walked out for his encore in his usual period clothing, his loin cloth. The band chugged through a nineteen-song set, nearly a third of it from the sluggishly selling *Done with Mirrors*. Russell made it to the Spectrum, and the next day told them so. Their cover of James Brown's "Mother Popcorn," he raved to Tyler, "was def."

If Saturday was normal, Sunday would be anything but.

"It was unlike any other recording session we had," said Rubin.

That, for the producer, was not a good thing. On one level, the day would be a thrill, almost surreal. Aerosmith was one of his favorite bands growing up. Now, at just twenty-two, he would be working with them. But so many other factors made the session uncomfortable, awkward, and frustrating.

Start with the location itself. This would be the first and the last time Run-DMC used Magic Venture Studios in Manhattan for *Raising Hell*. Their home base remained Chung King. Rubin still isn't sure why they ended up at Magic Venture. He wonders if it was more convenient for Tyler and Perry.

There was also the media presence.

MTV and *Spin* magazine sent teams to write about, film, and photograph the day.

Run felt more than a tinge of resentment about the added buzz.

"They didn't cover us," he said, "when we made 'Peter Piper' or 'My Adidas'"—both B-boy tracks and tracks that he preferred.

Strangely enough, DMC maintains that he didn't know about the session until the morning of it. He had been out partying at the World, the East Village club known for attracting everyone from Madonna to RuPaul to Keith Haring. When the phone woke him up Sunday morning, he wasn't thinking of going into the studio. He had something more important to deal with.

Over the weekend, Run had needed a car because his was in the shop. DMC was the only one with a credit card, so he helped Run rent a Lincoln Town Car with Budget.

"But because him and Jay smoked a lot of weed Saturday, Joe comes home and he leaves the key in the car and the rental car gets stolen," he said. "When I woke up and get the call from Joe, I'm like, 'Fuck the studio. I got to go find this rental car.'"

Did *Spin* and MTV find out about the session before Run and D? Possibly, though Jay had to be in on the plan. He was always the one behind the boards, next to Rubin and Russell, an unofficial third producer. Adler, the publicity guru whose Spidey senses seemed attuned to the macro, did not remember who told whom to go down to Magic Venture. But in addition to *Spin* and MTV, the band itself had local photographer Lloyd Nelson on hand to document the session.

Even if MTV sent a crew, there was no guarantee the video network was going to air anything.

"I was a bit dubious," said Doug Herzog, who supervised MTV News then and later became the president of Viacom's music and entertainment group, "because Aerosmith was a bit of a joke at the time."

Rubin, Cummings, and Sommer may have been friendly at that point. But the media presence, Rubin insisted, was not what he wanted. If he'd had control of the day, he would have had Tyler and Perry come to familiar surroundings at Chung King. He wouldn't have had anybody there to document it.

"Our mission was to make this music, and everything else that was going on there was really a distraction to the music being made," said Rubin.

Ideal conditions or not, the session proceeded as planned.

Rubin reported to Magic Venture in a black T-shirt with the Harley Davidson logo emblazoned in yellow. If you didn't look closely, you could mistake it for the Aerosmith wings.

George Drakoulias, his baby-faced NYU buddy in the *Breakfast Club* sweater, nervously waited in the studio. He was twenty-one, a year younger than Rubin.

"Are they going to come?" Drakoulias wondered out loud. "It's pre–cell phones, so there was a lot of anticipation. We finally heard they were downstairs, and we got everything up and running pretty fast."

Even if nothing came of the session, Tyler and Perry had one thing motivating them to scoot up to New York. They were being paid $8,000 for their guest spot. It's not clear if Tyler knew ahead of time that the moment would be documented, but he certainly dressed the part. He wore a red satin jacket over a T-shirt with a matching red scarf and headband. With his black jeans and matching sweatshirt, Perry could have passed for a B-boy—if he hadn't been a thirty-five-year-old guy from Massachusetts with a face as pale as steamed cauliflower. A glimmering guitar pick dangled from the chain around his neck.

Maybe, as they said later, nobody knew how it would turn out, whether they would even lay anything down on tape. But the media presence—and the extra bodies filling the studio—made it feel like something had to happen.

Rubin, Simmons, and Jay took their customary spots behind the board. In the twenty or so minutes of unscreened footage of the day in the MTV archives, you can get a glimpse of Beastie Boy Mike Diamond, still an unknown to the wider world but already a part of Rubin's inner circle, wandering around in the back. Perry would later claim that one of the Beastie Boys ran home during the session to grab him a bass to borrow. It's an odd thing to remember since Rubin, sober that day as always, didn't record a bass track or even attempt one as an experiment.

Danny Simmons, the oldest of the three brothers, took a seat in the back of the room. Russell had told him the night before that Aerosmith was coming and he was excited. "I had been a big hippie back in the sixties, been to see Jimi Hendrix concerts," he said. "Aerosmith, at that time, were a hair group, but just the fact that [Run-DMC] were creating a rock record with a legitimate rock band got me psyched."

Richie Supa also arrived, and not empty-handed. He and Tyler had more than music in common. They were drug buddies. "And I always came bearing gifts," Supa said.

The *Spin* article, published by Cummings, is surprisingly straightforward in alluding to what she saw in the studio that day. Never mind that Tyler and Perry had pledged in an earlier interview that they were clean after years of drug-fueled dysfunction. Cummings didn't hold back in her reporting. At one point, she describes Tyler's then girlfriend arriving with a jeweled cigarette case, "and they disappear into the bathroom and emerge noticeably refreshed."

Russell Simmons was more direct.

"What do I remember about Aerosmith that day?" he said. "They were in the bathroom a lot. They were sniffing a lot of coke."

Rubin decided to start the session with Perry.

The guitarist didn't go into a booth or separate room. That wouldn't work for MTV. Instead, he stood next to the board as he played a blond guitar with the words *Protect and Survive* branded into the wood.

"Joe didn't necessarily want to play the same solo as on the original," Drakoulias remembered. "And it was like, 'You've got to play the solo.' So we had to talk him into it. Had to coax him. And once he played that, we were just smiling."

Tyler stayed at Perry's side, beer bottle in hand. It was as if he could spot a camera a mile away and wasn't about to cede any of the spotlight to his musical brother, even if he wasn't supposed to be in the scene. While Perry played, Tyler hammed it up. He made hand signals in the direction of the engineer, thumb in the air, to turn up the guitar. He squealed the song's chorus into the air—there was no mic on Tyler—and improvised a short jive-talking rap of his own, punctuated by "Bless my soul, what it is. Nobody do it like DMC."

Perry wasn't putting on a show. He was playing. He stared down at his guitar, bouncing between the song's iconic riff and the chugging rhythm, in C, headquartered at the seventh fret.

"Joe Perry was brilliant," said DMC. "He just didn't say one word during the session. You would ask, 'Joe, are you okay?' He would just nod his head up and down. But when it was time to go in there, he walked in there, cigarette hanging from his mouth, winked his eye, they pushed record, and history was made. 'Joe, are you done?' He'd nod his head up and down and he'd go back and sit down."

The drum track had been laid down sometime before that Sunday. Typically, Rubin would put together five- to seven-minute loops as they built each song. That's what Perry played over. The guitar footage in the MTV vaults wasn't just for show. It's what ended up on the final recording.

And when Perry was done, he reached over the ashtray for the hard pack of Camels and lit another. Jay got up and moved to the other side of the room where his turntables were set up, across from the mixing board.

You can hear Tyler speaking in the background of the video.

"Is this still MTV?" he asks. "Unbelievable. You're getting some stuff here. Hot stuff."

If he only knew. Minutes later, Perry and Tyler moved to where Jay was standing and were watching him play "Walk This Way" on his left turntable. (A second copy was already on the other deck.) Jam Master Jay put on his headphones and went to work.

Nobody spoke. The Aerosmith front men stood to the side, in the frame, like a pair of gawky freshmen boys at their first high school dance. They were listening to their signature song reduced to its thirteen-second intro, the beat slashed and diced and shifted and scratched.

"That, to me, was the most captivating part of the day," DMC said. "He was going back and forth, cutting it up. Steven and Joe was just standing there, looking at him like, 'Yo.' They had no idea what we did with their record. But when you look at them, they were very respecting and open and present."

Were they trying to embrace Jay's approach, understand it, or just waiting until the next trip to the bathroom? It's hard to know.

"What Jay's doing is what we did ten years before meeting Aerosmith," said Run, describing the DJ's technique. "What Jay's doing right there is why they even got a phone call. And when Rick walked in and we were doing that, he said, 'I know that record. We'll make the whole thing over.' Huh? That's where the problem started, and that's where Russell said, 'Perfect,' and that's where me and D just did our job."

• • •

Did our job.

Dutiful, focused, professional. This was not standard operating procedure for Run-DMC. Well, maybe for Jay.

"Jay loved being a musician," said Run. "Loved, loved, loved all of this. Me and D, chipmunks. Let's get some beer, get some burgers, eat, be happy. I'm going to hurry up and do it like Jay said so I can get back to the burgers and pizza and weed and happiness."

DMC remembered exactly how they found themselves in this

spot. It still amazed him how the smallest choice, the slightest stroke of time and place, could change everything.

Click back to an earlier afternoon. Maybe it was March. Maybe it was even during the winter. DMC and Jay were in the studio, screwing around with "Walk This Way" on the turntable. Only, D didn't know it as "Walk." On Jay's record, the song title had been blacked out with a magic marker, that old DJ trick to keep other mix masters from stealing beats.

DMC was, as we've said, very familiar with that beat. So was anybody who had ever stepped foot in a park jam or popped one of Flash's tapes into a boom box. Hell, Flash laid that beat down as far back as 1978. DMC planned to let Jay work the turntables, and it would go something like this:

"It's 1986. I'm DMC. And the place to be. Been rappin' on the mic since '83. I'm the best MC in history. There will never be an MC better than me. That's why they call me the K-I-N-G."

Then Rubin walked into the room.

"Do you know who this is?" he asked.

"Yeah, this is *Toys in the Attic*, number four," DMC said.

Pause.

"He said, 'No, the name of the group is Aerosmith,' and proceeded to tell us its history."

In those days, there was no Genius or even Google. If you wanted to know about a band, you were told about it. And if you wanted the words to a song, you had to look at the liner notes. And if the words weren't in the liner notes, you had to listen to them and scribble them down.

Which is what Rubin told Run and D to do next. They

weren't going to just use the beat, he told them. They were going to cover the song.

He handed them a notepad, a record, and told them to go to D's basement.

"We go down to my basement and put on the record and then you hear 'Backstroke lover always hidin' 'neath the covers,' and immediately me and Joe get on the phone and say: 'Hell no, this ain't going to happen.'"

They hung up. Then they let it ring. It is impossible to know how long they refused to take a call. In some retellings, it's a week, though that doesn't make sense. Sometimes, it's just hours. Nobody knows for sure. What we do know is that eventually a call led to détente.

And the push came from Jay, the DJ who wasn't even pictured on the album covers, who, as *Spin* revealed later that year, had been getting a fraction of the song royalties that went to Run and D. But Jay was vital, the peacemaker whose role was not fully valued until he was gone and peace grew so hard to come by.

He finally got through and started talking to Run.

"Motherfucking Joey," Russell Simmons yelled in the background and grabbed the phone.

Run handed it to D.

"Darryl, you stupid motherfucker for following him," Simmons yelled.

Eventually, Russell handed the phone back to the DJ.

"Jay, where you at?" Darryl asked, not wondering about location, but wondering where Jay's mind was. There's something you should know, Jay told them. Rubin was working to get the guys on the record to come into the studio. The real guys from Aerosmith. Steven Tyler and Joe Perry. Then, the Sunday morning wake-up call. They're here. Come on down.

Jay gave the guys direction when they arrived.

"We know how you feel about those lyrics," he said. "Don't do the lyrics the way Steven done them. Do the lyrics the way Run and D would do them."

Even when they got there, Run and D were distracted. You don't see them on camera as Jay shows Tyler and Perry his work on the turntables. They were in another room, on a couch, devouring a bag of McDonald's burgers. They were also still dealing with "Budgie," trying to figure out how to resolve the rental car crisis.

Perry, thirty years later, remembered Rubin calming D down, explaining that he wouldn't have to pay out of pocket for a new Lincoln Town Car.

"'Don't worry about it. Insurance will cover it.' And finally Rick said, 'Hey, you guys, we've got Joe and Steven in here. Let's do something.' They were very ambivalent about this whole thing. He told us, 'I don't even know if we're going to get this on the record, on the album. But let's give it a try.'"

• • •

Before Run and D hopped on the mics, MTV brought everybody together for an on-camera interview. It's incredibly entertaining to watch, particularly if you appreciate the sort of tension you might find on an episode of *Curb Your Enthusiasm* or while watching a figure skater tumble during the Olympics.

They were gathered in three rows—Tyler and Perry in front; D and Run behind them; Jay, Simmons, and Rubin in the back.

You can't see the interviewer. She's got her back to the camera. But you can hear her. She's clearly coming to this cold.

Before they start, you hear DMC tell Run, "We're going to fuck it up, so don't worry about it." Then he was silent, as he always was during interviews in those days.

"Were you fans of Aerosmith?"

"Excuse me?" said Run with a blank stare.

"Were you fans," she repeats, slowly this time, "of Aerosmith?"

"We loved it," said Run. An odd choice of pronoun, except when you consider that he was talking about the song because, in all honesty, he had no idea what to say about these scraggly white guys he'd just met. "We liked the hard-core beat. We had to find something to rap over. This is before rap records is even made."

Jay cut in from the back, clearly recognizing Run's failure to follow even the most basic rules of press conference etiquette.

"Big fans," he said. "This is our favorite group."

Rubin looked over and broke into a laugh.

"Joe and Steve, were you fans of DMC?"

"Yeah, we've heard 'em," Tyler said, chewing frantically on his gum.

"I like their style, because there's a lot of electric guitar in it," Perry added.

"Finally," Tyler cut in weirdly aggressively and then looked over his shoulder at Run, who didn't acknowledge him but adjusted his Kangol.

"How is this version going to be different?"

"'Cause we gonna be on it," Run said.

And then D offered his lone on-camera quote.

"Yeah, we gonna be rappin'. Jay gonna be scratching. Like back in the D-day."

"What about the video? Can you tell me about the video?"

"What video?"

• • •

As much as they played nice for the cameras, they were not happy. Blame that on the "hillybilly gibberish."

Having Tyler in the room didn't change Run's and D's collective attitude.

Rubin knew this and it was just one more thing to sweat.

"I remember just thinking how Run and D didn't like the lyrics, and here's the guy who wrote the song," Rubin said. "I felt like I knew a lot of information that a lot of other people in the room didn't know, and it was making me uncomfortable."

Cummings captured this in the *Spin* article. At one point, Rubin told Run and D to work on the lyrics with Tyler out in the hallway. The Aerosmith singer obliged, even grabbing a marker to try to help scribble words down for the guys. They resisted. They were actually still talking about the rental car. The police had apparently located the Lincoln. They just needed to go down and reclaim it.

"I want it to be B-boy language," said Run.

"I keep telling you, it already is," said Russell.

"Hey diddle diddle with the titty in the middle," said Run.

"Hey diddle diddle with the *kitty* in the middle," corrected Tyler. "Get some paper and I'll write it down for you."

"No, that's okay, we know it," said Run. "We're just gonna do one take, then we gotta leave. We gotta return the car."

Years later, Tyler still remembered the nerve of those kids. He just let it go.

"What was I going to say?" Tyler said. "I didn't want to get into a big fight with the guys. I tried to show them a couple lyrics, and they got it, but it was clear to me, when I told them what the words were, that they were used to singing it their way and they wanted to sing it that way. When they said, 'Looking at T,' I said, 'T? You mean, me?' They said, 'No, T, man.' It was just one after another."

Later, the MTV cameras captured Run and D in the recording booth. They were facing each other, at the microphones, and nobody else was in the room.

Run wore a gray inside-out sweatshirt and his Kangol. D had on a black-and-red Adidas sweat suit and no hat. They started with a little improvisation. Run beatboxed the rhythm. D rapped.

"This is it, y'all. We make a record with Aerosmith, y'all. And it is def, y'all. It is def, y'all. I saw that Aerosmith is the fuckin' best, y'all."

As soon as the last "y'all" slipped out, D turned to the camera with the big schoolboy smile, as if he'd just hit the gym teacher in the nuts with a medicine ball.

"That is what we would have rather been doing over that beat," Run said now, watching the footage. "Just hanging out with my friend."

They moved on to the actual lyrics. There were no iPads, no assistants to walk them through the song. Run and D clutched the crumpled pieces of paper on which they'd scribbled the words. They were trying, but stumbling.

D took the lead most of the time. He stuck with "titty," not "kitty." Run basically kept quiet until they got to the chorus. They then rotated a series of lines that would never, ever make it onto anything resembling a released album.

Run: *Then the bitch said.*

D: *Walk This Way.*

Run: *Stinky crab said.*

D: *Walk This Way.*

Run: *Dirty ho said.*

Run took the lead for a verse, but things got worse. He was too hopped up, almost screaming into the microphone. He threw in a "motherfucker" without warning. He got annoyed and started rapping Just Ice's "Latoya," a popular rap hit from the day.

Then he tried "Walk" again. It wasn't sounding right. He was given instruction over his headset.

"That's not the way I rap," he complained, looking off camera to the production booth. "Why I gotta rap when it get hectic?"

By "hectic," he was talking about blasting guitars.

"I wanted to rhyme over Isht-Tat. Like back in the day." He waved a hand in frustration and looked away.

• • •

They got what they needed from Perry and Tyler by the time the session ended around nine p.m. Run and D, though, were going to have to try it again. That first, stumbling attempt wasn't going to work.

Rubin tried to reason with them. He didn't yell, just

explained why Tyler's original words, as much as they hated them, were actually a kind of rhythmic poetry if they could just open themselves up to it.

"There was certain phrasing in that song, the way Steven sang that song, that would actually benefit a rap version," Rubin said. "There were things about Steven's version that were actually better to rap than what Run and D were doing. More syncopated from what they were doing."

Jay was more direct.

"Jay yelled at Run and D and said, 'You're going to look like chumps if you don't come in and recut it,'" remembered Adler. "Jay got it on a musical level. He's a DJ, a music lover. You're going to get squashed if you guys don't come back into the studio."

So they returned.

Chapter 18

CRACKING RADIO, CRACKING MTV

Run-DMC had never had any problem with the critics, and *Raising Hell* would be similarly embraced. When it arrived that May, *Rolling Stone* hailed it as the "first truly consistent rap album." In concert, they remained a popular draw, selling out arenas not just in New York and Philly, but in New Haven, Richmond, and Jacksonville. The beauty is that, for a time, they could know that none of it had a thing to do with "Walk This Way." The first single off their third album had been "My Adidas," which sparked the first endorsement between a musical group and a shoe company. "Peter Piper" was on the flip side.

At the Apollo, in April, Run-DMC included those songs, and added two more from their third album—"Hit It Run" and the title track, "Raising Hell." They didn't play "Walk This Way," the strange cover song that somehow didn't feel like their own.

"It was a separate thing in my mind," said Run. "I was happy about 'My Adidas,' about 'Peter Piper.' I wouldn't think about performing 'Walk' in Charlotte, North Carolina, in front of twenty thousand black kids."

Until, that is, WBCN started playing "Walk."

The Boston radio station, 104.1 on the FM dial, was hugely influential dating back to the late 1960s, when it reformatted from classical to rock and counted future J. Geils Band singer Peter Wolf as one of its original DJs. While the station stuck to the standard rock format, programmers did have the freedom to push local bands. WBCN hosted an annual "Rock 'n' Roll Rumble" contest. It also pushed local groups like the Cars, 'Til Tuesday, and Boston. And WBCN developed an especially close relationship with Aerosmith, airing an early gig live and, years later, giving away thirteen thousand tickets to the band's Worcester Centrum concert to celebrate the station's eighteenth anniversary. DJ Mark Parenteau was particularly close with Perry, whether encouraging him to rejoin Tyler during the down years or just sharing drugs.

But the key to getting Run-DMC's version of "Walk This Way" into the station's rotation was Oedipus, WBCN's program director. Born Edward Hyson, he'd adopted his moniker during the 1970s while introducing American listeners to the Sex Pistols and the Clash on, of all places, the Massachusetts Institute of Technology's radio station. By 1986, he was looked to as a leader, somebody who could single-handedly spark a hit.

"Oedipus might have been the top, most respected programmer in the country," said Bill Stephney. "When he played something, others would fall in line and say, 'It's safe for this to play now in Podunk.'"

There was a routine at WBCN. Label reps came in on Mondays to present their new records. Tuesdays, the radio station's staff would hold a meeting to decide what to add to the playlist. In this case, Oedipus didn't remember needing twenty-four hours that July. They put the new "Walk This Way" on right away.

"For us, it gave us a new Aerosmith, Aerosmith refined, Aerosmith reinterpreted," said Oedipus. "And Aerosmith was our band. We broke that band, we played that band, long before me. So when we got the song, we were excited."

Before long, Run-DMC could feel that something had shifted.

"I got my Adidas sneaker, made out of pure gold, and performed every song on the album other than 'Walk This Way,'" said Run. "Then I hear this exploding on a rock station in Boston and I'm seeing sales that are taking it well over 1.5 million. The next time out, I started to play it."

A radio hit was good, but an MTV hit, by that point, would be even better. Plotnicki recognized that right away.

MTV was the key to turning Run-DMC from rap superstars to pop superstars. "My Adidas" wasn't going to do that. The single landed in the Top 10 of the black singles chart, but it wasn't going to crack the *Billboard* Top 40. To Plotnicki, "Walk This Way" felt like the best chance Run-DMC had to take a leap, to become rap's first superstars. And to do that, he knew they would have to crack MTV, and not just for an occasional play after midnight. They were going to need to find a slot in the music network's regular rotation. And that, for a rap song, wasn't just rare. It was unprecedented.

Consider how MTV launched just after midnight on August 1, 1981. The opening showed the countdown through an astronaut supposedly planting the MTV flag and the flat voice of John Lack, one of the station's founders, announcing the start of a new era: "Ladies and gentlemen, rock and roll."

There was nothing new about lip-synching for short clips to sell music. Elvis Presley and the Beatles did it on the big screen, rock bands in the '70s did it for the British program *Top of the*

Pops, and former Monkee Michael Newsmith created *PopClips*, a precursor to MTV, that sparked the first wave of videos, from the Rolling Stones ("Waiting on a Friend"), the Police ("Walking on the Moon"), and the Pretenders ("Brass in Pocket").

But MTV was a different beast, a twenty-four-hour network launched as cable TV spread through suburbia. The timing was perfect. As home entertainment took off—with everything from VCRs and Atari 2600 video game systems—MTV became the country's biggest sonic watercooler.

Video did not kill the radio star, as the Buggles song went, but it did have the ability to make the radio star look like a damned fool. For those who understood the new medium, MTV could also be a godsend, a direct line into living rooms without the competition you might find on the radio dial. There's a reason five of the first fifty videos played on MTV were by Rod Stewart and another five were the same Phil Collins clip, for his 1981 hit, "In the Air Tonight."

"We were desperate for music," said Les Garland, the ex-radio guy installed as MTV's head of programming. "I said, 'We should change this to the Rod Stewart channel.'"

That wouldn't be necessary. Video budgets soon became as essential as a tour bus for new bands, established icons, everyone. But Garland and his programming team faced a new kind of pressure. John Lack's original promise to deliver "rock and roll" spoke to MTV's rigid playlist. The station modeled itself after the dominant rock radio format—album-oriented rock, or AOR. And AOR meant REO Speedwagon, Starship, and Styx were going to dominate the airwaves. It also meant black artists, particularly those that fell outside traditional rock radio, were going to struggle to make the rotation.

This came to a head during Michael Jackson's revolutionary rise in the early '80s. Jackson's *Thriller*, produced by Quincy Jones, marked his transition from boyhood star to one of the most dynamic performers of the modern pop era. As the story went, that didn't matter to MTV. The network refused to play Jackson's "Billie Jean" video at first. Until CBS Records head Walter Yetnikoff threatened to pull all of its artists off the video channel. MTV buckled, Jackson became the first video superstar, and the color barrier was broken.

Except, once again, legend is not the same as truth. It's very hard to know for sure whether the "Billie Jean" incident actually happened or, if it did in some way, the details got jumbled as the result of a bad case of telephone.

Garland said that MTV was desperate to put on Jackon's video and that it was a no-brainer. He insists he got into an argument with Yetnikoff over another CBS artist, Barbra Streisand, who he refused to put in the rotation.

"It drives me beyond crazy," said Garland, "because it's just not true. There was never a question of us playing Michael Jackson, there was never a question of us playing 'Billie Jean.'"

Carolyn Baker, MTV's former director of talent and acquisition, called Garland "a colossal liar" and talked of being brushed off when she pushed the idea of a James Brown special on MTV. Brown, she argued, was at the center of the move from rhythm and blues into rock and roll. No, she was told. As far as MTV's audience was concerned, rock and roll started with the Beatles.

"It is an issue of racism," Baker said. "It was an issue of racism. The channel was racist."

Mark Goodman, the first VJ to appear on MTV that early morning in 1981, falls somewhere between Baker and Garland. Early on, he found the format frustrating, but not surprising. The guys running MTV all came out of radio, and in radio, you stuck to the format.

"And that format was a rock format," he said. "Nobody called WPLJ in New York, where I worked before, and said, 'Why aren't you playing Michael Jackson?' It was a rock channel. But as things moved forward, it musically didn't make any sense. I don't really think the people who were programming were racist. I just think they were shortsighted."

There's one thing beyond debate. If by 1986 some black pop stars had become MTV stars—Jackson, Prince, Aretha Franklin—most of the artists in heavy rotation were white. Journey. Jon Parr. Night Ranger. And rap? It simply wasn't in the mix. The few hip-hop videos that existed were played rarely and at odd hours.

Plotnicki didn't have to go far to find the creative answer for "Walk This Way." Profile's offices at 1775 Broadway were in the same building as Jon Small. In the late '60s, Small had played drums in two of Billy Joel's early groups, the Hassles and Attila. As MTV grew, he had become one of the industry's most successful video directors. He and Joel, eager to diversify the network, made a particular effort to add black actors to the pop star's 1983 video for "Tell Her About It." In 1986, Small produced another video hit with Whitney Houston's "Greatest Love of All."

"That's why we went to see him," Plotnicki said. "He got a black artist on MTV."

At Profile, Plotnicki had already developed a fascination with the network. He had been particularly hands-on with "Rock Box" and "King of Rock," viewing the videos as a rare opportunity to broaden the group's audience, and the not-so-subtle ingredient seemed to be old white men. Professor Irwin Corey would be the first face you saw in "Rock Box," the aging comedian rambling through a monologue meant to discuss the meaning of rap. On "King of Rock," Run and D jog up to the front door of a fictitious museum of rock and roll—the Rock and Roll Hall of Fame wouldn't open until 1995, for another decade.

"You ain't gonna believe this place," Run said.

"Word," replied DMC.

"You gonna bug," said Run.

And as soon as they walked in, they were met by an elderly white security guard played by Calvert DeForest, known for playing Larry "Bud" Melman on *Late Night with David Letterman.*

"This is a rock and roll museum," DeForest told them. "You guys don't belong in here."

It was an inventive, electric, and funny video. It also got a lot less airtime than Mr. Mister.

Small wasn't naive. He told Plotnicki there was only one way a Run-DMC video was going to get heavy play on MTV. He had to get Tyler and Perry to be part of the shoot.

• • •

Tim Collins warned Small right away. Tyler was going to try to take control of the shoot. He would try to change everything.

"Just ignore him," Collins told him. "Do what you do."

To say that Aerosmith wasn't excited for the video era would be an understatement.

"We didn't want to do videos," said Perry. "We thought that it took away from the magic of the music. It kind of defined what your song was rather than using your imagination. But we decided, 'Let's do one.' It sucked."

That's not exactly true. Even if Aerosmith's clip for "Let the Music Do the Talking" wasn't about to get confused for Fellini, it wasn't any worse than what passed for video gold in 1985. Jerry Kramer, with Rod Stewart and Styx videos already on his résumé, follows a group of superfans intent on sneaking video equipment into a gig to bootleg their favorite band. Kalodner has a cameo, working some sort of drive-up photo booth, and the final scene, for reasons unexplained, ends with the kids watching their secret footage on the couch with the actual members of Aerosmith.

Two weeks before the shoot, Small decided to call up Tyler to explain his concept for "Walk This Way." Tyler admitted he was worried.

"Just don't make fools of us," he told Small. "I don't want people laughing at us."

"He knew they were in a tough position," said Small. "They hadn't been out there in a long time. And in my mind, I wasn't even sure they were going to air it. I know I said to him, 'If anybody's going to laugh, they're going to laugh at the other guys.' I never saw it as a fun video or a joke video. I always saw it as a serious performance where two groups join each other."

Small developed the concept after a few listens to the song.

It wasn't subtle. Tyler and Perry would be jamming in one room. Run-DMC would be hanging in another. The only thing separating them would be a wall. And when Run-DMC began the first verse of "Walk This Way," the music would overpower their "neighbors," eventually forcing a frustrated Tyler to smash a hole in the wall. Physically and metaphorically, the wall between rock and rap—between white and black—would come down.

As excited as Profile was, it was still Profile, which meant this wouldn't be a special effects bonanza. Small got a modest $67,000 budget and did his best to stretch his cash. He found an old, closed-down theater in Union City, New Jersey, for the shoot. He decorated Aerosmith's side of the wall with a few '80s pinup posters and had a very pregnant Billie Perry and Tyler's future wife, Teresa, sit behind them. Run-DMC's room was bare, a lightbulb hanging from the ceiling, a Whodini record on the wall, and Jay's turntables. Early on, Small decided to recruit three members of the local band Smashed Gladys to serve as a kind of fake Aerosmith rather than fly in Whitford, Hamilton, and Kramer.

If there was any resentment among the three of them about the recording session in March, there was merely resignation about the video shoot.

"Certainly, I guess if I really wanted to be there I could have taken out my credit card and gone up, but I didn't," said Whitford. "We had misgivings about it, that we weren't going to be included. But we had no idea what it was going to turn into at that point, either. It was kind of, 'Ah, man,' because so many times in this band the focus has always been on Joe and Steven. It was just another 'Here we go again.'"

Small needed to fill the theater for the post-wall segment, when the two groups would perform together. So he had local radio stations announce the shoot and the need for an audience. When he and his crew reported to work that June morning, there was a problem.

The kids outside were mostly African American. The crowd was supposed to be there for Aerosmith. It turned out he had his stand-ins. The trouble is, the white kids were in their cars.

"They were scared to get out," said Small. "Rap wasn't big then. It was never on TV. So with a bunch of assistants, I knocked on the windows of the cars and told them to go to the backstage door. There were probably about two thousand kids. They came in first. Then we started to shoot. And from all the black kids who were hanging out in the doorway, they could hear the music and hear everything, and they eventually broke through the glass, pounded it, and came in. It was crazy, almost like a riot."

There are varying accounts of Tyler's and Perry's states while making the video. It was June, so they were months away from rehab. Collins, who wasn't there, got reports that they were shooting up and making everybody wait. "Total nightmare," Collins said.

Small didn't remember any of that. "They were pretty coherent," he said. "They had their security guard with them, and Tyler came in carrying a huge medical book that had every pill in it."

The dynamic between the two groups was, Plotnicki remembered, "beyond chilly." He overheard Tyler and Perry worrying about their absent bandmates.

"They were worried that the rest of the guys in the group

were going to be pissed off," said Plotnicki. "They were worried about the shoot. 'Make sure it doesn't look like Aerosmith.'"

Bart Lewis, the Smashed Gladys' lead guitarist, was also struck by the almost total lack of interaction between Run-DMC and Aerosmith.

"Steven almost went out of his way not to be involved with them," Lewis said. "I thought it was kind of weird he spent as much time talking to me and ignoring them. I think maybe it was a music business thing. Somebody's riding somebody's coattails and each of them think it's the other. Aerosmith is thinking, 'This song is going to make you guys huger stars than you are.' They're thinking, 'They're going to get a comeback based on doing this with us.'"

The ice did seem to break as the hours went by.

Around 3:00 the first morning, Small looked over at Run and Darryl, sitting, their heads touching, exhausted. Tyler came over and shouted, "Wake up, wake up."

"Why are you so up?" Run said.

"I eat pussy every day," Tyler shouted back. "That's what gets me so up."

• • •

They didn't look like they belonged in the same room. Run-DMC were wearing what they always wore: All black and unlaced Adidas sneakers, flaps out. Tyler dressed as he usually did: He wore body-hugging tights, a long, flowing shirt open to reveal his bare chest. Perry placed a lit cigarette in his headstock as he pretended to play guitar.

That first day of shooting started early and stretched for

more than eighteen hours into the New Jersey night. Small shot the video out of sequence. His first shot was of the silhouetted Run-DMC in the back of the stage before they bust out into the Aerosmith gig. On day two, Small focused on the two rooms and the wall.

"Small was a genius," said Tyler. "It was his idea to build that set and put the wall up. And he said, 'I'll saw a hole in the wall and you just hit the spot.' If you watch the video, the way I go up and fucking try to smash and knock a hole through the wall, it didn't budge. Whoever was supposed to saw it didn't really saw all the way through. It just about rippled every muscle in my back."

Small laughed when he heard this.

"He hit that thing like a ton of bricks," he said. "It wouldn't have been good if it broke, one, two, three. It had to have a little tension in it."

At MTV, it wasn't a given that "Walk This Way" was going to get on the air.

"It wasn't like we were waiting for the next Run-DMC record," said John Sykes, the network's cofounder. "I don't think we knew Run-DMC."

But they knew Aerosmith, and Les Garland, who oversaw programming, remembered the day the video rolled in.

"My office was a full-on dance scene," he said. "I think I remember putting it on the next day."

The video was an immediate hit, whether you liked rap or hated it, whether you cared about Aerosmith or considered them washed-up '70s dinosaurs. It was hard to deny the joy of what Small captured.

"That video, I still think it's hysterical," said Nina Blackwood, one of the original MTV VJs.

Bill Stephney also noticed. He was working with Public Enemy on *Yo! Bum Rush the Show*. Their debut wouldn't be out until early 1987, a record inspired by Run-DMC's crunch, but with a political edge.

"As much as some folks will look back at the video as being corny, that's really what happened," said Bill Stephney, a founder of Public Enemy and later the president of Def Jam Records. "Suddenly, it's okay for young black men and young white men to have a relationship culturally."

Even rockers who didn't care for rap found themselves drawn to the video.

"When I saw the black guys with the black shirts on and the funny hats, I kind of got it," said Eddie Money.

When Tommy Shaw of Styx saw the video, he admits he felt threatened.

"But at the same time you couldn't help but sing along to it," he said. "It was pretty brilliant. Everybody's thinking, 'Why didn't I think of that?'"

• • •

On the morning of September 13, 1986, a perfectly clear day, Doug Herzog left his apartment in the West Village and hopped into his Honda Accord—MTV actually gave him a car allowance—for the hour-long drive to his cousin Jon's wedding in central Jersey. He had just turned twenty-seven, and his gig at 1775 Broadway was going well. The MTV News team, his crew since his hiring in 1984, was a hit. He had led the department's

Live Aid coverage, and even pitched in with on-camera interviews of Lionel Richie and Dionne Warwick. Sometime that spring, as part of the regular MTV News coverage, raspy-voiced VJ Nina Blackwood narrated a ninety-second segment on the day Perry and Tyler met Run-DMC in the studio.

Jon and Karen's ceremony took place at the Martinsville Inn in front of an almost-all-white crowd. The groom wore Chuck Taylors to make a point. He'd been in a punk band in high school and had agreed to wear a suit, but only if he could punctuate it with those black sneakers. The groomsmen were given *Risky Business*–style sunglasses. Then there was the music. Jon admitted he was a bit of a snob. The last thing he wanted was a cheesy wedding band. Instead, he hired a DJ and gave him a stack of records with yellow Post-it notes marking the songs to play.

He and Karen's song would be the Style Council's "You're the Best Thing"—definitely obscure enough to deliver that "we're not like everybody else" message. But a wedding is a wedding. And the DJ also dug into the matrimonial party canon: Billy Idol's cover of "Mony, Mony," Sister Sledge's "We Are Family," and Kool and the Gang's "Celebration."

And right there, in the middle of the mix, without a pause, the DJ pulled out a now two-month-old single by Run-DMC. The floor thumped and, by the end of the record, Jon and the guys, decked out in their shades, were dancing on the parquet floor with arms locked, simulating the half-cool, half-awkward movements emblazoned on their brains from a summer of MTV.

So much would happen in the next twenty years for Doug Herzog. He would greenlight *Yo! MTV Raps*, *The Real World*, and *Beavis and Butt-Head* before moving on to Comedy Central and starting *The Daily Show* and *South Park*. One day he would become president of Viacom's Music and Entertainment group and be inducted into the Broadcasting & Cable Hall of Fame alongside such luminaries as Walter Cronkite, Lucille Ball, and Oprah Winfrey. But for some reason, for Herzog, there would always be something special about that September in New Jersey when the DJ at his cousin Jon's wedding played "Walk This Way."

Chapter 19

WHO IS THE KING?

On November 4, a month after "Walk This Way" departed the Top 10 and less than two weeks before the Beastie Boys' debut *Licensed to Ill* would be released, the weekly *Village Voice* delivered a cover story on Rick Rubin. It wasn't just any story.

"KING OF RAP," the headline declared in big, bold type below a large photo of the bearded, long-haired producer and small snaps of his most recent projects, Run-DMC, the Beastie Boys, and LL Cool J.

The author of the article, Barry Walters, made no bones about it. He opened his Rubin profile by referencing Phil Spector, the Wall of Sound revolutionary who would be recognized as one of the most influential figures in pop history. Rubin was "the closest pop music has come this decade to producing a conceptualist who can compare to Spector in studio wizardry, business acumen, and steam-rolling ego."

These days, when newsprint is considered an endangered species, it may be hard to understand the impact of a *Village Voice* cover. But in 1986, the weekly was a crown jewel of the alternative press that had emerged during the cultural foment of the late '60s. Scoring a cover was a big deal.

Back at the Rush offices, it did not go unnoticed.

Bill Stephney, who had been hired as Def Jam's first

employee, largely to sign Public Enemy, admitted he was, in part, looking to playfully josh Simmons by calling to let him know his partner had scored the cover. Simmons didn't get the joke. He sent out Jimmy Spicer, "The Bubble Bunch" rapper who was now working at Rush as a messenger, to a newsstand to get him a copy of the *Voice*.

Later that day, Stephney stopped in to see Simmons at his office on Elizabeth Street. The paper was on his desk.

"He was livid," Stephney remembered. "He despised not only being presented as the business promo guy, but also the marginalization. That Rick was getting all the credit for the hipness of Def Jam and its cutting-edge, sort-of-punk feel."

As upset as he may have been, Simmons didn't say anything—at least publicly. He left that to his younger brother.

In a response published two weeks after the cover story, Joseph "Run" Simmons from Hollis, Queens, took the unorthodox approach of writing a letter to the editor that was critical of a flattering profile of his group's producer. The letter was headed "You Be Illin'."

"About y'all calling Rick Rubin the King of Rap—he's not," Run wrote. "If anybody's the King of Rap, it's Run-DMC, and if it's not us, it's my brother, Russell Simmons, who's charted twenty-one singles this year, and currently has seven singles and five albums on Billboard's national charts.

"Rick Rubin is not just a very close friend of mine, he's a great multi-talent deserving of a claim. But it fucks me up that anybody thinks that he made my album. When I write my lyrics, I write the music and the final mix at the same time, and that's the motherfucking truth!"

• • •

"Of course it was bizarre," said DMC. "Rick, deep down inside, knows he didn't invent the shit. He worked with us on what we were creating."

But D wasn't about to write a letter in protest.

"Look, Run, he's that person," said DMC. "He's not going to let a motherfucker take a shine. I didn't give a fuck. The shame about it is this. Larry Smith is the King of Rap. Rick came along and *Raising Hell* was so big that people forgot about the motherfucker who did 'Rock Box' and *King of Rock*."

Rubin, for his part, viewed the cover two ways.

"It was ridiculous," he said. "I think also the fact that I was for the most part at that time the only white person added a level of confusion to it."

Still, it was hard to deny that, for Rubin, who had old issues of the *Voice* stacked up in his room back in Lido Beach, making the cover was incredibly satisfying.

"The *Village Voice* was the magazine that I read every week, so it was a surreal experience for me," said Rubin. "To be on the cover of that and the pictures in there with your parents, I mean, it was a big deal. But I didn't really comprehend how other people felt about it. And no one ever discussed it with me."

He remembered the letter. He couldn't remember if they ever talked about it.

"I would bet almost anything, Russell did not tell Rick how he felt," said Bill Adler, the Def Jam director of publicity. "What might have been the adult thing would have been for Russell to let Rick know how fucked up that was. But I'd be surprised if he did. Likewise, if you think about it, I really wonder what all did he say to Larry Smith when that moment came when he's being pushed aside in favor of Rick. I would bet he had nothing to say to him."

Run-DMC and Simmons did have a legitimate beef over the amount of credit Rubin found heaped his way for *Raising Hell*. On LL's *Radio*, he had titled himself the "reducer" rather than producer, and had been largely responsible for taking a teenager's ideas and raw energy and turning them into a comprehensible audio record. LL made it clear that *Radio* couldn't have been made without Rubin.

"He was in every step of the way," he said.

On *Raising Hell*, the dynamic would be different. Rubin was working with experienced rappers who had recorded two successful records, mingled with Dick Clark, and been the only rappers to play Live Aid. Run-DMC also wasn't a group with a formalized production process, with established pecking orders and rigid rules in place.

"You know, we were all friends and everybody says what they think, and the artist does with it what they want," said Rubin. "In some cases, a homeboy could have more influence than a producer, depending on the person. The fact that I was quote-unquote producer didn't give me any more power than Runny Ray, their friend who would hang out in the studio with us sometimes. If Runny Ray said something and if they liked what he said, that's how it would be."

That's not to downplay the significance of Simmons bringing in Rubin. Even if he never touched a knob or picked up his guitar—even if he never said a word—bringing in Rubin was, in itself, a production decision. It meant that there was a certain aesthetic he wanted on *Raising Hell*, an aesthetic in line with the punch of "It's Yours," *Radio*, and "Sucker M.C.'s."

But the issue of credit does get sensitive when you ask Run.

"I wrote *Raising Hell* on the road," he said. "When I got to the studio, I could make five records a night, me, D, and Jay. 'You Be Illin',' 'My Adidas.' Whatever. Four or five records a night. Rick come in. He had ideas. Me and D probably got tired and leave. Him and Jay reshape it, fix it, but the ideas were laid out."

DMC said that, for him, there are two major moments that show Rubin's influence on *Raising Hell*.

The first was obvious, just the fact that they decided to cover "Walk This Way" and not simply rap over the beat. The second was subtler. It was about something that was simply natural, an ability to know when to touch a track and when to leave it alone.

He brought up the recording of "Peter Piper."

In the third verse, DMC kicks in with "Jay's like King Midas, as I was told / Everything he touched, turned to gold."

"After we laid that down, I hated it because the rhyme didn't match the intensity of the opening with me and Run," said DMC. "It was all laid-back, relaxed. I was like, 'Yo, Rick, I got to change it.' So he was trying to see if he could not have me change it. Rick tells me, 'All right, come in tomorrow at eleven a.m. I'll be here. You could change your lyrics.' So eleven rolls around, I show up. I go in there and I yell it.

"Rick calls me up to the booth and sits me down. He said, 'This is what you did last night. This is what you did right now. You tell me which one sounds better.' And for some reason, the one I did last night sounded better. So Rick was like, 'You can go home now.'"

So back to the King. It is, said LL Cool J, who has never shown any bitterness, any resentment, any frustration, at least publicly, about the African American journey in America, why you never hear Bruce Springsteen or Madonna or even Mick Jagger called "old school." But the term's thrown around for any rapper over forty.

"The media is funny," said LL. "You have some people that want to, you know, have a coronation and crown Rick the King and say I never did anything. That Run and D never did anything. You can't really fight that. I don't really think like that. When it comes to credit and media attention, people have a tendency to respond to people they can relate to. You probably had a lot of media guys who can relate to Rick. Then you have those who understood what we brought to the table."

Chapter 20

NOT FOR $200 BILLION

And suddenly, it was 1987.

For Aerosmith, that would be the year everything turned to gold.

"That song gave them hope," said Tim Collins. "And that song was also where they went, 'Ah, Kalodner was right.' And they listened to him. They listened to him for three solid albums."

First, they had to clean up. Collins brought in Dr. Lou Cox, a clinical psychologist.

"I know at one point Tim hired a former DEA agent to try and manage the buying and distribution of drugs in some controlled fashion with Joe and Steve," said Cox. "But addiction, by definition, is out of control. And no matter what you do to get that person to control it, they can't. And that's what they finally came to recognize and realize."

Aerosmith gathered in Collins's office in Cambridge early one morning. They had to do the intervention before Tyler used that day. So they lied to Tyler, telling him that the BBC wanted to do an interview on the success of "Walk This Way." With London five hours ahead, the video hookup required the early start.

It wasn't pretty. Tyler felt he was being singled out. He was. Perry also needed rehab, but he had been given permission to wait until Billie Joe, pregnant with their first child, delivered the baby.

"He thought he was coming in to do an interview with the BBC about 'Walk This Way,'" said Collins. "One of my guys went to get him. He came in to do the interview and he said, 'What the fuck is this?'"

The intervention worked. Tyler took to the treatment, as did Perry, and then the other guys.

Newly sober, they stopped fighting Kalodner.

"Tyler felt I interfered with his music," said Kalodner. "He said in many interviews that his music were his children and I killed his children."

Now they listened. They agreed to work with slicker producer Bruce Fairbairn, fresh off Bon Jovi's *Slippery When Wet*, a record that had sold twelve million copies. They traveled to Vancouver to record at Fairbairn's studio. They also agreed, for the first time, to work with a group of professional songwriters, including Desmond Child, Jim Vallance, and Holly Knight. "(Dude) Looks Like a Lady," which Child helped them write, arrived in September, becoming the band's first Top 20 hit since—you guessed it—the rereleased "Walk This Way" in 1976. "Angel," another Child cowrite, rose to number three.

Permanent Vacation, the band's ninth studio album, went on to sell five million copies, remaking Aerosmith as MTV darlings and returning them to football stadiums. If the sound was a little glossier, the edges smoothed over, so what. One of America's most popular bands had been reborn, and the new model became even more popular than the original. Aerosmith's next two records, *Pump* and *Get a Grip*, were also with Fairbairn and even bigger than *Vacation*.

The year started out strong for Run-DMC. After six months off, they headed out that summer with the Beastie Boys on the Together Forever tour. They were on the charts. They had their $1.6 million Adidas deal that, as much as the cash, marked the rise of hip-hop merchandising as a central revenue source. Whether Dr. Dre selling headphones or 50 Cent holding a bottle of Vitamin Water, rappers were now commercial commodities.

If there were issues during the rise of *Raising Hell*, they were mainly about the cultural disconnect or misunderstanding between this suddenly wildly popular genre of music and the mainstream, with white media fumbling around trying to cover it.

Fights broke out, either in the arena or in the parking lot, and the press blamed Run-DMC. If those writers and TV talking heads had been paying any attention, they'd have realized that the concerts were not the cause of the conflict but merely the opportunity, a place for acting out in gang-infested cities. But by the summer of 1987, with the Beasties and Run-DMC packing arenas from Honolulu to Philly, hip-hop's first supergroup seemed perfectly positioned for the long haul.

That's when something shifted. It started with a lawsuit.

Russell Simmons had been grumbling about Profile for years. He hated the deal they signed in 1983, and now, with his own label and the clout of the Beasties and Public Enemy behind him, he believed it made almost no sense that his signature group, the group with his brother, was stuck with Robbins and Plotnicki. Simmons wanted Run-DMC set free. Maybe another small label would have allowed a buyout, but Robbins and Plotnicki were not patsies. They were business-savvy, unforgiving, but not crooks. Bullying, in the press or in court, wasn't going to convince them to let their signature act go.

Plotnicki, in particular, believed too many small indie labels made the mistake of selling off their biggest assets. Sign a group, support them through the early days, and then let them fly when they get huge. A deal was a deal, he said. He wanted to hold on to Run-DMC.

So, in the summer of 1987, Simmons sued Profile for nonpayment of royalties.

Profile countersued and froze Run-DMC's accounts. The label also froze Run-DMC. Simmons was never able to prove that Profile had cheated him, and the case would eventually be settled. But the damage had been done.

There had been an ambitious, multipronged plan to follow *Raising Hell* with an album and Rubin-directed feature film called *Tougher Than Leather*. Adler, at the same time, would publish the group's authorized biography branded with the same title. In the end, as Simmons and Profile battled, only Adler's book would come out in 1987. *Tougher Than Leather* would be shown to the world for the first time in 1988 and bomb. And by then, the film's director—and their producer—was gone.

Rick Rubin's exit, like his arrival, seemed utterly unscripted.

He had earned his film and television degree from NYU's Tisch School of the Arts in 1985, despite nobody seeming to remember him cracking open a textbook. The diploma created a short-term problem. Rubin needed a place to live or, more important, to run Def Jam. By now, Simmons, with business booming, had moved Rush's offices from 1133 Broadway to a former ballet studio on East Nineteenth Street. Lyor Cohen, who had come east to take a job at Rush, moved into the space with Simmons.

"The relationship between Rick and Russ," said Adler, "was always pretty complicated. It was really sort of a ménage à trois."

Bear in mind, the guys themselves would never talk in those terms. They later admitted differences over visions for the company and artistic direction—particularly when the Beastie Boys started drifting from Rubin toward Cohen—but talking about feelings and loyalty and friendship would have taken them to a place none were equipped to go. To mature adulthood.

In Adler's eyes, the flashpoint came when Rubin and Simmons spent about $1.5 million to purchase and renovate a five-story building on Elizabeth Street. The idea, as Rubin understood it, was that he and Simmons would move in together to live in the upper levels and the Rush and Def Jam offices would be on the ground floor. The geographic proximity would bring them together and make it impossible for them not to spend time talking. Rubin even had a recording studio built in the basement.

"Then Russell never moved in," said Adler.

That started the split.

The clear differences in taste didn't help. Rubin, still a rocker at heart, decided to produce metalheads Slayer and the Cult, a slicker band that he dosed with a harder-edged, AC/DC sound. Simmons's passion was for R&B, and slushy R&B at that. He signed Oran "Juice" Jones and Alyson Williams.

The Beastie Boys situation did not help. It had been a triumph that had somehow turned into a conflict.

Rubin had worked with the Beasties on *Licensed to Ill* for more than a year. When it came out, just before Thanksgiving

1986, the record became an immediate smash. *Licensed to Ill*, soaked with attitude; samples from Led Zeppelin, Black Sabbath, and Joan Jett; and even a song cowritten by Run-DMC, would be the first rap record to hit number one.

But instead of reveling in success and recording a quick follow-up, the Beasties began battling Rubin and growing closer to Cohen. They would eventually leave Def Jam, putting out their sophomore record, *Paul's Boutique*, for Capital. That wouldn't be until 1989.

Adler could sense the tension early in 1987. He had taken a leave from Def Jam to write Run-DMC's authorized biography. Simmons, strangely enough, was hard to pin down for an interview. For weeks, he tried ineffectively to get his boss to talk with him. When Simmons finally did, at an Alyson Williams session, the mogul seemed frazzled.

"Bill," Simmons said. "My Jews are fighting."

How much they fought or how much they simply internalized is unclear. Rubin wasn't a screamer. He was barely around the office, anyway. And no matter how much he and Simmons disagreed—on Lyor's meddling, on whether to partner with major labels, on why the fuck you would want to put out that Juice Jones bullshit—they never let tempers flare. Looking back, maybe they should have. A few hard but honest discussions may have actually helped keep them together.

Late during the summer of 1988, Rubin, Simmons, and Bill Stephney, who was now running Def Jam, met at the Empire Diner in Chelsea to discuss the future of Def Jam. Again, no shouting, no attacks.

"Do you want to leave the company?" Rubin asked Simmons.

He said he didn't.

"Then I guess I have to leave the company," Rubin said.

"I felt like the kid who was trying to figure out whether he was going to live with Mom or Dad," said Stephney. "That was the closest I'd ever seen to any confrontation. But it wasn't. They were literally like a married couple, two ships passing in the night."

Stephney would remain in New York with Simmons and Cohen. Rubin would head to California, where he'd launch Def American Recordings and become the most successful music producer of his time, a man whose portfolio swept across asshole rock (Red Hot Chili Peppers), hip-hop (Jay Z, Kanye West), metal (Danzig, AC/DC), Americana (Avett Brothers), and the revived careers of Johnny Cash and Neil Diamond. Eventually, Def American became American Recordings. With a theatrical flourish, Rubin had the Reverand Al Sharpton oversee the funeral of the word "def," a term he forever left behind.

Could Rick Rubin have guided Run-DMC through changing styles and dynamics as George Martin did the Beatles? Could he have kept them current and also kept them together?

Rubin himself described his exit much as his arrival, as if Scotty beamed him in and out of Chung King.

"We never had a falling out," he said. "There's never any bad vibes. We never discussed it. It just sort of happened. I think they sort of, if I remember correctly, they just sort of did more self-producing. It's not like they got a new producer. They just sort of continued on their own without me, if I remember correctly."

Dan Charnas, who worked for Rubin after he headed to California, had his own theories on the split.

First, there was the larger question of how Rubin viewed production. He had always been an adviser, a curator, a style maker.

"He is not a knob turner as a producer, just as Russell Simmons is not," said Charnas. "He listens to a song and an arrangement and sees the gems in it and polishes those and suggests ideas at key points, which elevate the production. We tend to conflate production with musicianship, but some of the greatest production ever is simply enhancing. To me, he rests more in the enhancer area. He is a performance coach. He works in song craft."

Which is to say that, in 1987, it would have been easy for Run-DMC to downplay the significance of a performance coach. Remember, this was before Rubin worked with Tom Petty or the Chili Peppers. As of *Raising Hell*, he had really only done LL's first record and "It's Yours."

"And Run-DMC were superstars," said Charnas. "If Rick Rubin decides to leave Def Jam and work on heavy metal records and stay in the Mondrian, Run-DMC are not going to cry about that shit. Because they are grown-ass men and they produce themselves."

The filming of *Tougher Than Leather* did not help. Rubin, the director, lost interest early on, stopped coming to the set, and created a subpar final product. Reviews were poor. The film lost money. Then there was the Profile lawsuit, a "terrible mistake," said Cory Robbins.

"It got them off track," he said. "I think it did more damage to them. I think it did damage to Run's psyche."

It also cut Profile off from Run-DMC. Robbins admits he doesn't really remember talking about Rubin's exit back then. In fact, he's not even sure he knew.

"They made *Tougher Than Leather* while we were fighting, so we weren't really in on it," he said. "I don't remember that we really heard any of it until toward the end of the lawsuit. Jam Master Jay walks in two shopping bags of master tape and said, 'Here's our new album.' I'm like, 'Really?'"

The pressure had particularly been getting to Run. Everybody thought he was suicidal. The Rush side said that's why they settled. Robbins and Plotnicki have their own explanation. That it became clear that Profile hadn't cheated Run-DMC.

But by then, so much had happened. Public Enemy. Boogie Down Productions. Ice-T. Eric B. and Rakim. All made their debuts in 1987.

Eventually, in May of 1988, *Tougher Than Leather* came out. It wasn't a bad album, with a thicker sound stuffed with samples and a lone song produced by Rubin, a remake of The Monkees' "Mary, Mary." But sales of *Tougher Than Leather* lagged well behind *Raising Hell*, coming in just over one million copies.

"We thought it was going to be huge, we thought it would sell more than *Raising Hell*," said Robbins. "It didn't."

• • •

Everyone said it. Questlove, approached in the hallway of *The Tonight Show*, was asked about Run-DMC. "If only those guys could work it out. They're leaving millions on the table."

After *Raising Hell*, there were highs. Run-DMC's 1993 record, *Down with the King*, updated their sound and landed them on the charts again. The 1997 Jason Nevins remix of "It's Like That" hit number one in England. But by the end of the 1990s, bad feelings had set in. DMC had also lost his voice and struggled with depression. He barely rapped on *Crown Royal*, their seventh album, released in 2001.

The next summer, there was a triumphant opening slot on an Aerosmith arena tour. Every night, for an encore, Tyler and Perry would call Run-DMC back to the stage, where they'd celebrate their grand collaboration, performing "Walk This Way" together.

But those gigs marked the effective end of Run-DMC.

On October 30, 2002, a little over an hour after sundown, somebody came to see Jam Master Jay in the Queens recording studio he was working in. That somebody shot and killed him, sparking a deep period of mourning and also of speculation. Was Jay, perpetually in debt, killed to settle a financial score? Was it just a random beef that led to the crime? The questions would be unanswered. After more than a decade, the murder would still be unsolved.

"If Jay never got killed," said Marvin Thompson, his half brother, "the group would still be going strong today."

Maybe that's true. The Eagles did it, through gritted teeth. So did Guns N' Roses, Van Halen, and even the Everly Brothers, who despised each other enough to once break up during a concert. They joined another feuding band couple, Simon and Garfunkel, to play packed arenas decades after their last hit.

Darryl heard this all the time, from everyone. He had an immediate answer. He'd do a show here and there with Run.

"But you could pay me two hundred billion dollars," he

said. "I'm not touring with Run and I'm never, ever making a record with him."

"There's an old saying, man, and it's cheesy and a little corny, but it's true," said LL Cool J. "Ego is not your amigo. My thing with them is that I respect both of them, and I respect D's feelings completely. The problem is, if one of them was to go away or pass away, god forbid, they would realize what they gave up. You're sacrificing something just for a feeling, an emotion, a principle, something you've established in your mind. You've dug your heels in on something and you're denying the world—us, your fans—the opportunity to see you guys."

So as the thirtieth anniversary of *Raising Hell* approached, LL had an idea. He would get his onetime mentors back on the road, and not with a handful of club gigs, but an arena tour worthy of kings. LL didn't know much about D's money problem, the fact that, in his most desperate moment, he had sold his publishing revenue stream to Steve Plotnicki. He just knew that Run and D, for all they had done, were letting their legacy drift into the history books. The one-offs were fine, and LL had done a gig with them in 2014 at the Barclays Center in Brooklyn. What LL had in mind was something different.

They would head out for forty dates, celebrating the most important rap group in music history at the perfect moment, the anniversary of their greatest record. This would give fans a chance to celebrate their heroes, introduce the duo to a new crowd, and also deliver a fat paycheck. Run and D deserved that.

LL wasn't going into this blind. He knew the guys, he knew

the minefields. He came up with a plan. Money would be a consideration. So would respect. It didn't matter that James Todd Smith, since those days in Hollis, had sold millions of records, hosted the Grammys, even became a regular on CBS's *NCIS: Los Angeles*. To make this work, everything, he decided, would have to be equal.

"I had millions of dollars on the table," LL said. "I had set it up perfectly. Because their fee was going to be split, and I'll take half of their fee so we could all make the same amount of money, as men, to our families, and we were going to go out."

Performance order came next. When the Everlys reunited, they opened for Simon and Garfunkel. That made sense. They were clearly not the headliners. But even if the former James Todd Smith had ruled as Ladies Love Cool James since he was a teenager, even if he remained a central cultural force, he knew how to be humble. He would open for Run-DMC.

He met separately with each, making his pitch to Run and D.

"I wanted to be respectful," said LL. "And I'm just being honest. 'Yo, you all go on last.' I just felt like that was the right way to do it. We were from the same neighborhood. They came out before me, and I felt like I didn't need to be closing on Run-DMC. That was how I felt about it out of respect, for who they are as a group. It's not that I can't close. But I respect them that much. You guys close, you guys go on last. I'll go on right before you every night. Let's do what we gotta do."

The summer got closer. Run was open, willing. D was willing at first, at least it seemed so. Then he started to waffle. He didn't like the money. Then, that was fine, but he didn't like playing so many dates. Okay, they cut back the calendar. Then he wanted to open up the shows with his rock band.

Dates began to drop off. Soon the tour became thirty cities, then twenty. Eventually, LL had to accept that his grand plan wasn't going to come together.

"They just strung it out and strung it out and strung it out until we had to cancel the whole thing," said LL. "We couldn't close the deal. I couldn't close the deal."

"I don't hate Run," Darryl said.

But he couldn't let what happened slide. When he lost his voice, when his drinking got out of control, he considered suicide. At the moment, the only person he remembered reaching out to him was the man most everybody else had cast as the villain: Steve Plotnicki.

By now, Plotnicki had split with Cory Robbins and, not surprisingly, with a nasty lawsuit of their own. Plotnicki won, of course, and sold the label to Sony in 1998 while holding on to its profitable publishing arm. Plotnicki heard about DMC and paid for him to get into treatment. He also offered him a quick financial fix. He bought out D's publishing revenue stream. The cynical would consider that taking advantage of a man who was down. But DMC maintains that selling to Plotnicki was what rescued him when he had hit the lowest of lows. When nobody else was there.

Run certainly didn't reach out to help. He made a solo album, *Distortion*. A solo album executive-produced by Russell.

"He's the one that left," said Darryl. "We went to war together and we was in the midst of the battle, and when the battle got fuckin' heated, people was falling to the left and falling to the right of us. The helicopter comes. Joe can walk. Joe's not shot. Joe's not injured. He jumps up in the helicopter. The captain of the helicopter looks at Joe and says, 'I don't think we have room for one more.' And he looks at me lying down there bleeding and bloody in the bushes and Joe says, 'Take off.' And that's what happened. And he took off. He went about his way. And I'm lying there bleeding to death, and I realized I'm the only motherfucker that's going to get me out of this shit."

As he got to talking, it was clear it wasn't just that moment. It was everything. Run-DMC, Darryl said, had no reason to exist after *Raising Hell*.

"Run-DMC should have done what Cream did," he said. "We should have broken up after that third album. There was nothing left to do. If Rick would have stayed, what happened with *Tougher Than Leather* would have happened anyway. *Raising Hell*, from 'Walk This Way' to 'My Adidas' to 'Peter Piper' to 'You Be Illin',' that's all we had as a group collectively. We toured two years off of *Raising Hell* and then we put out *Tougher Than Leather* and hip-hop had completely changed."

Something had also changed within him. He had spent all that time as the silent one, letting Run and Jay take control. Now DMC wanted a voice. He came to them with ideas. They dismissed them. He remembered one of them, "Chill to the Mill," and can still rap it today. They stopped listening to him and he started drinking, more and more.

"Run-DMC was still making bullshit when PE and De La and Tribe and Big Daddy Kane come along and was putting

EPILOGUE

The first time I talked to Run was in early 2016. It had been a struggle to get him on the phone. His assistant told me, at least a dozen times, that he was simply too busy to talk. The breakthrough came when I made it clear I had already spoken with DMC, Russell, Rubin, and virtually everyone else in his musical history. That's always the key to dealing with a celebrity as a journalist. Nobody wants to get to the party first, but when they hear who else is on the guest list, they grow desperate to be in the room.

My first chat with Run wasn't particularly deep. He was available only on a day I was traveling. I took his call, during a short layover, halfway down Terminal C at the Charlotte Douglas International Airport. I could hear Run all right, as I cradled my cell phone on my shoulder and banged out the words on my laptop, but some words were definitely lost. He did tell me enough to help me connect the dots for the original *Washington Post* piece on which this book is based.

It would be another year before we talked again. This time, the delay wasn't purely the Rev's tight schedule. A dispute over royalties with his former publishing company had created a cloud over our interactions. Run's manager felt I was going to focus on his business. I said I needed to have a deeper talk and agreed not to press him about the royalty issue, which was part of a court case. The conversation would be centered on "Walk."

I walked into an immaculate house and waited in the living room. Run came in wearing a black Adidas sweat suit. He looked heavy, though not quite as heavy as I'd seen him in the past. His head was shaved and he greeted me without a smile, but with a handshake. I told him I'd brought something special, the nearly fifteen minutes of unreleased video from the Viacom vaults showing the March 9 session. I hoped we could watch it together.

Run was everything I'd hoped for. He didn't pretend to be my friend. He did commit to the process. When I asked a question that he felt dragged on too long, he would raise his hand and wave me quiet. He closed his eyes and rubbed his forehead as if channeling a part of his brain rarely accessed. It was dramatic or melodramatic, but that was fine. I was sitting with Run, and we were going back in time.

If you listen to him directly, the interview became an almost extemporaneous blend of narrative and word association.

We watched one scene on my laptop as Perry played his guitar while standing next to Tyler at the soundboard. Jay was there, sitting next to Rubin, but Run and DMC were nowhere to be seen.

"I remember some of this guitar stuff going on," he said. "I was around this. I didn't care to be around this stuff long."

I came back to Jay. Why was he in the thick of it?

Press pause, Run told me.

"The answer's very simple. Me and D, kids running around, didn't care about making this record. Jay loved being a musician, loved being a DJ. Loved, loved, loved all this. Me and D, chipmunks. Let's get some beer, get some burgers, eat, be happy. What does Russell have us doing? Jay, like he's supposed to be, is in his job. We're bad kids. Mischievous kids. And Jay stayed for the whole session like he's supposed to. And we mischievous kids. Then they tell us go home and learn the lyrics. Why? We gonna making this record over. Wha?"

It goes like this for most of the next fourteen minutes.

We watch as Jay stands over a pair of turntables in the studio, seemingly giving Tyler and Perry a tutorial on how he used their original song. How he bounced from one record to the other, not letting Tyler's voice enter the mix. Press pause.

"What Jay's doing is what we did ten years before meeting Aerosmith. He's showing them what we did. This is what Jay's doing. What Jay's doing right here is why they even got a phone call. And when Rick walked in and we were doing that he said, 'I know that record. How do you know it? We'll make the whole thing over.' Huh? That's where the problem started, and that's where Russell said, 'Perfect,' and that's where me and D just did our job."

Not much I've told Run on this day impressed him. The fact that I've got every obscure record (Jimmy Spicer! Orange Krush!) from back in the day. That I've talked to virtually everyone you could track down, from the icons (LL and Rubin) to guys he hasn't heard from in years. I tell him I had lunch with Eddie Martinez out in Oregon. It doesn't bring even a smile. But this video, that's something special.

"This is the most fascinating tape on the entire earth," Run tells me after it's all done, and then he sits back, closes his eyes, and who knows what he's thinking about.

ACKNOWLEDGMENTS

Ideas are everything and David Malitz is the one who suggested I do an oral history of "Walk This Way" for the *Washington Post* back in 2016. Liz Seymour gave me the freedom to "think big," a tenet of her leadership. And then there is Christine Ledbetter, the best editor a writer could have. She can line edit, brainstorm ideas, or talk you off a ledge. Marty Baron has been my big boss for fifteen of the last seventeen years, an inspiration at the *Boston Globe* and now at the *Washington Post*. He doesn't just say arts and culture matter but has a ticket to the symphony.

I am so grateful to be at the *Washington Post*, which is packed with talent and kindness. Some of the colleagues, friends and editors, past and present, who have been invaluable: Amy Argetsinger, Amy Hitt, Mitch Rubin, Matthew Callahan, Caitlin Moore, Erin O'Connor, Michael Johnson, Suzette Moyer, Magda Jean-Louis, Greg Manifold, Tracy Grant, Alice Crites, Emilio Garcia-Ruiz, Jim Webster, Tom LeGro, Cameron Barr, Alexa McMahon, Tim Carman, Ron Charles, Liz Whyte, Sam Martin, Karen Heller, the great Peggy McGlone, Fiona Luis, Scott Heller, Suzanne Brown, J. Peder Zane, and Brooke Cain. I am so glad Jessica Alpert Silber, the great audio juggler, continued to take my calls and we were able to make *Edge of Fame* together. Jeremy Rosenberg's creativity remains an inspiration. Patrick Healy has always supported and boosted everything I do. He is family.

Peter Guralnick, Tom Perrotta, and Alan Light read an earlier draft of the book. My hope is that the book is 30 percent as good as the pieces they've dashed off on a Thursday afternoon.

My parents, Karen and Lewis Edgers, have supported everything I've done. Same for my sister, Liz, who is always publicizing my stories. My uncle Bruce's first guitar and stack of '60s records opened my teenage universe. I'm lucky enough to have a second family that's as supportive as the first. Thank you for that, Jack, Bonnie, and Donna.

My wife, Carlene Hempel, is the only person I ever want to impress. There is no more deflating feeling than reading a draft to her out loud and realizing it's flat and no better feeling than when she tells me it's working. Her generosity toward others stuns me every day. Lila puts up with my need to convert her to everything, from Pavement to Public Enemy. She the funniest person I know. Calvin's embrace of his turntable, his piano playing, and his demand to spend every waking hour listening to Harry Potter audiobooks keep us smiling.

There are so many people who gave me time for this book. That was key because in this clip-job, repurposing society, I pledged that every quote would come from my interviews. That simply wasn't possible. Some people have died. But 98 percent of the quotes are from people I spoke with.

Darryl McDaniels always took my calls, even for minor fact checks. It took a while to get to Joe "Run" Simmons, but when I did, he sat patiently on his couch and emptied his mind and heart. Bill Adler's Rolodex, knowledge, and generosity have led to an entire area of scholarship. Thanks to Bill Stephney, Tim

Sommer, Ben Ortiz (with Cornell's incredible Hip Hop Collection) as well as Check the Technique's Brian Coleman.

Jack Douglas and Tim Collins helped connect multiple eras in Aerosmith-lore. So did Steven Tyler, Joe Perry, Brad Whitford, Tom Hamilton, Rick Dufay, and Joey Kramer. Please YouTube Jimmy Crespo so you can hear how he plays.

David Rosenthal offered me a book deal without my even proposing a book. He learned of the original *Washington Post* story while I was plugging him for interview sources. I was blessed with two fabulous editors. Brant Rumble took this on, offering creative and practical guidance. Jill Schwartzman inherited me but made me feel like the firstborn, tightening and shifting and focusing the end, in particular. Rick Richter, my agent, demystified the process of book publishing and always went to bat for me.

PHOTO INSERT CREDITS

(in order from top of page to bottom)

PAGE 1
Bill Adler Archive at the Cornell Hip-Hop Collection
Manny Bella/Bill Adler Archive at the Cornell Hip-Hop Collection
James Hamilton
James Hamilton

PAGE 2
Charlie Ahearn
Charlie Ahearn
Judy Sitz

PAGE 3
Talib Haqq
Talib Haqq
Michelle Charters

PAGE 4
Courtesy Tim Collins
Ricky Powell
Ricky Powell

PAGE 5
Mark Weiss
Ron Pownall
Ron Pownall

PAGE 6
Ron Pownall
Ron Pownall
Bob Wallin

PAGE 7
Mark Sawicki
Lindsey Anderson
John Harrell

PAGE 8
Courtesy Tim Collins
David Salidor/Bill Adler Archive at the Cornell Hip Hop Collection
Danny Sanchez

ABOUT THE AUTHOR

Geoff Edgers is a journalist and author. He is the national arts reporter for the *Washington Post*, and his work has appeared in *GQ*, *Spin*, *Wired*, *Salon*, and the *Boston Globe*, among others. He also produced and starred in the 2010 documentary *Do It Again*, and he is the author of multiple children's books about The Beatles, Elvis Presley, Stan Lee, and Julia Child. He lives in Boston with his family.